A Where

Jess

Angels

Fear

Ritual Abuse in Scotland

Also by Laurie Matthew
Who Dares Wins
BeAware

# Laurie Matthew

# A Where Angels Fear

Dundee
Young
Women's
Centre

"this
book is hereby
dedicated to
the colour
**GREY!**"

A Vip Publication

Author © Laurie Matthew
First Published 2002
by
Young Women's Centre
1 Victoria Road
Dundee
DD1 1EL

ISBN  0 - 9539961 - 4 - X

Designed by DM Graphics
Printed and Bound in Scotland by
Woods of Perth Ltd

# Contents

# Acknowledgements

This book is dedicated to the many unknown and unrecorded child victims of ritual abuse. It is for those countless children, who never knew life, love or hope, those who were never allowed to draw first breath, those who knew only a brief life of too long suffering and those who never knew anything other than pain and abuse.

Some of these unnamed victims I have been told about and each and every one I have named and taken into my heart. Though I never knew them, I will never forget any one of them. For them, the least I can do is try to make the world more aware of some of the abuses that go on and on, fogged in perpetual secrecy.

Thanks are due here to the many brave survivors who have, despite their own suffering, told me of these victims, it has made them real for me. The only time I ever wish that I could find a way to believe in a loving God and a heaven waiting to welcome these children is when I think of those tiny people who never had a chance.

Thanks are also due to the survivors who have shared their lives and their memories with me over the years, and the many dedicated workers who have worked with me to provide support services for survivors of abuse. All these amazing people have leant me strength and helped to keep me almost sane.

Thanks also to my five children for giving me the time and space to write, bringing me back, occasionally, to the real world by their constant demands to be fed and watered at regular intervals, and for generally putting up with me while I work.

*Thank you Bill and Nicole for your proofreading skills. I promise to try and learn to spell before I write the next book.*

## Introduction

**This book is the natural follow on from the last publication concerning ritual abuse produced by the Young Women's Centre** and entitled, *'Who Dares Wins.* Those who have read *'Who Dares Wins'* have described it as an easy to read, informative and very practical book for helping survivors. This book hopes to be more of the same.

A great deal of material has been written about ritual abuse, which I haven't managed to find the time to read yet. This is because, being a simple soul who only wants to help survivors in a  practical and supportive way, I find most books to be too academic or too focused on therapy for my simple tastes. The truth is, I can't always understand the big words used. While there is definitely a great need for these books, and I am certain that they help many survivors and the practitioners who work with them, given that I found the books too academic, I looked around for something a bit simpler.

After a few years of finding nothing simple enough for me, I decided that maybe there was a gap in the reading materials. I then made the decision to write some very practical books to provide valuable information and help survivors, their non-abusive family and their supporters.

There is a great deal missing from *'Who Dares Wins'* and also from this book. This is due to the fact that I have tried very hard to stay away from the more sensational side of the issue, and have also been determined to bring in the survivors' perspective without using any of their experiences or exposing them in any way. Their stories are their own, and they may write them for themselves someday if they ever choose to. In my opinion it is not my place, nor is it my right, to write another person's story.

If anyone is hoping to read horror stories in this book, forget it. They quite simply are not there. I have deliberately stayed as far away from describing gory details as I possibly could. The examples I have provided in this book, to try and clarify some of the events, are simple examples. Everything else can easily be left to human imagination. The only way to hear the real horror of what goes on is to build trust with survivors and listen to them.

My aim in this book is to expose the abusers and their actions as much as possible, and to provide as much information as I possibly can about how the whole thing works, what they do, how they do it, what it does to the survivors and how people can help survivors. As I have absolutely no credibility to start with, it cannot be lost through believing in survivors and writing about ritual abuse as a live issue in Scotland.

I make absolutely no apology for believing that ritual abuse happens in this country, as I know beyond any doubt that it does. In this book, like the previous book, I will not enter into the usual debates as to whether or not ritual abuse happens and where on earth the proof of it all is. I personally have all the proof that I need in listening to, and working with survivors, and if anyone is searching for proof or that type of debate, you will definitely not find it in this book. All you will find here is information about the subject gained through many, many years of being with and listening to survivors.

Ritual abuse is an emotive subject and hearing about it or reading about it, particularly in detail can be extremely distressing for many people. Having said that, living with the abuse is distressing for the survivor, as is the painful process of trying to talk about it. As I have no intention of causing anyone any difficulties, this book is very carefully written so as not to cause distress to anyone (except hopefully some of the abusers).

Ritual abuse is a broad subject, very complex and not all of it can be described fully in the general way that this book talks about it. My particular experience lies mostly with survivors of satanic ritual abuse though I also have some experience of working with survivors of other abusive cults. I have tried to be general in my approach to the subject in this book to try and maximise the numbers of survivors who might be helped. No matter the belief system that survivors are abused in, the effects are often very much the same and abusive groups all tend to operate in much the same manner. At the end of the day, often only the names of the group and its associated paraphernalia change.

**I hope you will find the information contained in this book useful and interesting but mainly I hope that it will not sit gathering dust on a shelf but actually be used to help survivors.**

If you have read this book and no longer use it, pass it on to someone who will make some use of it. Feel free to contact me if you want to ask more specifically about anything in this book or the previous one, or if you think that I am missing out something absolutely vital. I can always explain more fully in the next book.

# Where Angels Fear

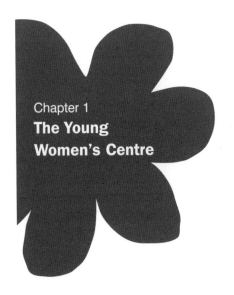

Chapter 1
**The Young
Women's Centre**

**The Young Women's Centre** is a voluntary organisation based in Dundee, but works with young survivors of abuse across Scotland and even, these days' parts of England. The Centre has been in existence since 1994 and over the years has supported thousands of survivors of different kinds of abuse. The Centre provides long-term, confidential support to young people, aged 18 and under, who have been sexually abused. The basic idea is to provide young people with a high level of support as soon as possible after disclosure or even while still living with the abuse.

The Centre encourages young survivors to take back control of their lives in a healthy and positive manner and seeks to minimise damage to the survivor. Getting help while still young can help stop the abuse from recurring, help prevent the many problems encountered by some adult survivors, reduce mental health problems, reduce criminal behaviour and help the young survivors grow more easily and safely into adult life.

The Centre works closely with a wide variety of statutory agencies and other voluntary agencies to provide the most effective package of services for individual young people, and their families, if this is appropriate. In the Centre, the young person is always viewed as the main person and remains fully in control of the service that they receive. They dictate the pace, decide what they want from the service, decide if they want regular appointments or whether to just drop in and see someone. They are generally regarded as the ones with the most expertise in their own selves and they are the people with their own answers.

Centre support workers are there to support young people in sorting out their problems for themselves, not to be any kind of expert who knows better than the young people what they need or want. Young people may not always know what they need or want for themselves when they are in crisis but with a little support, they soon get there and are perfectly capable of making good decisions for themselves.

In addition to the support services, the Centre is dedicated to preventing abuse from happening in the first place and ending it sooner. To this end, the Centre has developed the VIP Project. This project now has a range of abuse prevention materials available to suit all ages and stages of children and young people. The wee vip's is aimed at children aged four to six and their parents; the Tweenees is aimed at children age five to thirteen; the Teen VIP's is aimed at young people aged fourteen to eighteen and is also suitable for adults.

The Young Women's Centre has produced a wide range of resources and information aimed at raising general awareness, educating others about violence and abuse and helping young survivors of abuse to get help and recover from the trauma. These resources are listed at the back of this book and all are available from the Centre.

The Young Women's Centre provides training and talks for a wide variety of individuals, agencies and groups in order to share the many things we have learned about working with young survivors with as many people as possible. We are dedicated to changing the lives of young people for the better, finding ways to improve services for young people and ending abuse at all levels of society. Young people are our future and if they are provided with the information they need now, they will be better prepared to run this society and make the world a better place in the future.

# Chapter 2
# Working with
# Survivors of
# Ritual Abuse

Chapter 2
## Working with Survivors of Ritual Abuse

**I have been working with survivors of ritual abuse for more than twenty years now** and everything I have learned about this type of abuse I have learned first hand from the personal accounts of survivors. Over the years, I have found myself extremely privileged to be allowed to share many journeys of healing as survivors I have known have battled to escape their group and then struggled to stay free from the group and the associated abuse. For some it has been a long and extremely hard fought war, with many battles won and lost along the way. Many of these survivors are still fighting. For others they have fought and won and come out of it on the other side to live their lives free from fear and abuse. Some, a few that I have known and greatly admired, never made it at all but that made their battle for freedom no less worthy a fight. I mourn those few I have known who did not survive.

I have listened over the years to many survivors' painful attempts to break the long enforced silence. I have heard their words as they struggled to speak them aloud, witnessed their incredible drawings when they could not speak the words, read their writings when they could not speak or draw and even supported some survivors in approaching the police and other agencies for help. Always I have believed them. I have never had any reason not to do so. Few could ever witness such a struggle in any person to communicate and overcome extremes of fear, and not believe the words spoken by those survivors. The vast majority of those survivors who have spoken to me had never spoken to another living soul before me.

Nothing could ever be gained by survivors through talking to me, other than the intense pain of breaking the silence. I have no duty to pass information on to anyone, nor any ability to try and affect a rescue attempt. I can do nothing at all with any information given to me by a survivor and survivors who talk to me invest their trust in me as a person. I am not a therapist, I do not help anyone recover any memories and have no answers for anyone. My job is simply to listen. Survivors talk to me mainly to begin the process of telling and to have someone who will listen to them. They have never had this before.

Sometimes it has been very painful to watch survivors try to come to terms with their lives and learn how to try and live in a different type of world. Few realise just how difficult it is for ritual abuse survivors to adjust to the rules and beliefs of an entirely different culture and belief system. For many it is like being dumped in a strange foreign country with little or no resources to depend on, and a whole set of different laws and customs to learn, but with no one to teach them. Many times I have watched them turn back to the familiar, despite the abuse associated with it, as they could no longer cope with the newness and strangeness of a different way of life and culture. The miracle is that they ever try getting away from the abuse and that so many succeed.

As so few people believe that ritual abuse even happens in this country, these survivors of ritual abuse even have to contend with having their own reality denied to them. Those who do believe ritual abuse happens and are able and willing enough to listen and offer help to survivors are too few and often too hard for the survivors to find. Yet, somehow the survivors still keep on trying to find help and rarely give up. Such is their incredible will and determination to survive that they keep on going through set back after set back in their struggle to get away from abuse and get the help and support they need. Many are dragged back into the group each time they try to escape but still some of them keep on trying until they succeed.

Some of those incredible survivors have found their way to me and I have tried to help them as best I can. I am certainly no expert in anything, let alone this, but I do try to listen to the things that people want to tell me. On many occasions survivors approaching me have spoken about how often they have been let down by services and agencies which initially offered to help them.

Some of these agencies initially indicated that they could help and then further down the line gave up on the survivor, betrayed confidence or simply said that they could no longer help them as it was outwith their area of expertise. From what I have gathered, much of this has been due to some of the myths surrounding survivors of this kind. For example, some agencies still consider survivors to be dangerous and buy into the fear in such a way that they end up letting the survivor down in the end or imposing artificial boundaries and barriers on these survivors. Such a let down makes it all the harder for survivors to trust another agency and inevitably delays their healing. Sometimes it drives the survivor back to the group, as they cannot cope with yet another let down.

It would be better if some agencies learned more about ritual abuse in the first place, stopped assuming that all survivors of ritual abuse are the same and stopped making promises that further down the line they find they cannot keep. It would also be better if they did not fear working with survivors or mistrust them so much. Trust is very much a two way street, and the survivor is the one who has, for good reason, to work the hardest at it. It would certainly be better for survivors if they were treated as individuals with feelings and the same rights as everyone else, rather than being lumped together as ritual abuse survivors and therefore become classed as somehow different from everyone else. Survivors feel enough differences as it is without anyone else increasing the difficulties for them.

Many survivors do talk about getting good support from places such as some rape crisis centres; young people's crisis centres and survivors' telephone help lines. The common factor in what is generally perceived as good support isn't always having a great knowledge on the subject of ritual abuse. Rather it is not limiting the survivor to only an hour at a time to try and talk or limiting the number of times a survivor can phone or be seen by someone. It is not making promises that cannot be kept and is often simply listening to the survivor talk without making assumptions or judgements about them. It is being warm, honest, human and approachable rather than being distant, professional and aloof.

Survivors of ritual abuse are not all that demanding when it gets down to it. Many of them just want someone to be there for them and to listen and care about them as individuals. They want people to be honest with them and to treat them fairly. They want people to believe them when they talk and for people to take the time needed to allow trust to be built. They do not want any more than anyone else.

I have on many occasions worked with survivors who were still involved in the group and were trying to find help and support to help them get out. Although working with these survivors often means working at the sharp end of the fear continuum and has sometimes involved listening to extremes of current and ongoing abuse, plus raised many difficult dilemma's around child protection issues. This work has never been much different from supporting survivors of other kinds of abuse, neither has it ever placed me in any real danger. It has though, on many occasions, led to me having to try practising my very limited skills of FIRST AID.

Many people believe that the abusers will seek out and terrorise those people who are trying to help survivors escape and many even believe that survivors will, willingly or unwillingly, lead a supporter of theirs into danger. Many people believe that survivors will report back to the group with details about them and thus they may somehow become endangered. This, in more than twenty years of supporting and working with survivors has never been my experience. I suppose it is possible that abusers have sometimes been told, willingly or unwillingly by survivors, about me, but as I have nothing much to hide, so what! I would rather the abusers knew that I am against them and for the survivors. I do not have any problem in them knowing that I stand against them openly and will always make every effort I can to help the survivors and stop the abuse and those who carry it out.

I have on occasions entered the homes of survivors armed only with my fully charged mobile phone and my somewhat tarnished air of innocence and successfully led survivors out of the house right past the abusers. Some of those survivors later returned to the home and the abuse, some did not. I have even gone into a house immediately after a severe and life threatening attack on a woman by group members. Although the men knew that I was on my way as I had already phoned and spoken into the answering machine to say I was coming out to visit, only the woman was there when I arrived. The knowledge that all five foot two of scary me was heading to the scene, made eight brave men turn tail and run.

On that occasion, the abusers were in such a hurry to leave the scene of their crime that they left a great deal of evidence behind them, including the very badly damaged woman and the various implements they had used on her. One such device was still attached to her body. The only way I could persuade this woman in the end to allow me to call an ambulance for her was to clear all the evidence away first. This took a while to do but was necessary as the woman was more afraid of the medics seeing the proof of Satanism than she was of dying. This woman was in intensive care for a week and nearly died of her injuries but still she would not, or could not, name her abusers. With support, she later succeeded in leaving the group.

Although I have on occasions received threats from abusers, been followed both on foot and in my car, received abusive calls to my work and home and on two occasions actually walked into a very frightening set up, I have never personally been attacked by those abusers. I have learned that abusers depend on threats and fear and when these do not work, they give up. The survivors I have worked with have always gone out of their way to protect me and I have never felt at particular risk from their abusers. In order to safeguard survivors, I have on occasion even taken them into my home if I could find nowhere else in the short term to place them. Again, this has never led to any situation of danger to my family or myself.

I have found that although the abusers pose a very real threat to the survivors, they tend to use tactics of fear and intimidation to try and frighten people into panicking and stopping support of the survivor. I have personally gone out of my way to make a real nuisance of myself amongst local groups and have not worried about them knowing my identity, they have never yet attempted any direct harm to my family or myself. Then again, I am very public about what I do in my fight against this so-called non-existent crime, so to attack me would only give some credence to the fact that what I say is true, that they do exist. I have even dared them, but still they leave me alone.

There are many who might say that I am foolish, reckless, or as I once heard from a self proclaimed expert **'just been lucky so far'.**

I disagree completely. While I might agree that I am more than a bit foolish on many occasions and will even agree that I probably do receive much more than my fair share of luck, I am never stupid when it comes to personal safety. I am also an excellent judge of character and have no more reason to distrust a survivor of ritual abuse than I have to distrust any other survivor of any kind of abuse. Trustworthiness is nothing to do with whether someone is a survivor of a particular kind or not. I am very clear that it is the abusers who carry out the acts of abuse and violence, and they definitely prefer to stay hidden under the rocks rather than face up to the likes of me, armed with my trusty mobile phone, which is ever ready and willing to summon the local constabulary.

Strangely, in all my years of working with countless survivors, male, female and children, I have only ever found myself to be in any real danger when responding to some ongoing domestic abuse situations. I have worked with rape, child abuse, domestic abuse and ritual abuse survivors and come into contact occasionally with the different abusers, yet only with domestic abuse, up until now anyway, has the abuser ever been prepared to have a real go at me. Although I have always managed to get out of these situations before anything really serious has happened, each of them was bizarre, very frightening and potentially a high risk to personal safety. I would not say that luck got me out of these situations either though, rather I would attribute it to my being fairly cautious, quite perceptive, very quick to realise what was unfolding before me and being very timely about making a sharp exit. I've even been known to shift gear and run like hell on some very rare occasions.

In my personal experience, there have been several situations in which the abusers were told quite a bit about me and the survivor has even colluded with the abuser to set me up. Every one of these occasions to date has involved domestic abuse situations. Though I am always very careful of my own safety and the safety of others, the possibility of some risk does always exist when working with abuse of any kind. Yet, I would still, based on my own experience, regard getting involved in domestic abuse situations as being a bit more dangerous than getting involved in any other kind of abuse.

Survivors have honoured me with their trust over the years and I have always tried to be careful to keep that trust. I realise just how hard it is for survivors to place their trust in anyone and I feel that the least I can do is keep my side of the bargain. Confidentiality is one of the most common demands from survivors and I feel that they have every right to expect it from support services and from me. Having said that, there are occasions when I have faced huge dilemmas because of it. Often I have sat late into the night in total conflict with my conscience and sense of morality and wrestling with the difficult knowledge I have held in trust for a survivor. Sometimes I have wished that I could simply make use of that knowledge and just go in with the police and pull a survivor out. Always though, I have remembered the trust placed upon me and sat it out. It is not my place or my right to make the decisions for survivors. Survivors take time, and need that time to do things for themselves, and supporters can only wait in the wings, give support and hope for the best. It is not always easy to wait but then I remind myself that I am not the one who is living with the abuse.

The many survivors I have met and come to know have all contributed to making me a better and more enlightened person. I only hope that in return I have given them something. I have witnessed inner strength greater than I ever knew could exist in any one person. I have seen courage greater than could ever be displayed on any battlefield. I have met endurance almost beyond the human capacity to endure. On top of all of that, despite all the evil done to them, I have seen the goodness shine out from the survivors like a light that can be repeatedly dimmed but can never be extinguished. Perhaps the single most powerful thing I have seen in survivors of ritual abuse is the capacity to still be able to love and care about others. I have all too often seen survivors put aside their own suffering for a while to care for other people. I have to say that I find it totally awesome and absolutely inspiring.

I have learned a great deal from survivors of ritual abuse over the years and still have an awful lot of learning to do. Not only have I learned a lot about ritual abuse and the terrible things that are done to survivors, but I have also learned a lot about abusers and about human nature. I have learned much about the extreme badness of people and the human capacity to do evil, but I have also learned that even amid badness and evil, the seeds of goodness and right can take root and grow. I certainly do not know even the half of it yet and probably never will, even if I live another hundred years, which by the way is something that I fully intend to do.

*I cannot come close to saying that I have heard all there is to hear about abuse, or pretend to know all there is to know, and I still remain open to hearing and learning more from survivors.*

*Some of what I have learned about ritual abuse is shared in this book.*

# Chapter 3
# Ritual Abuse

Chapter 3
**Ritual Abuse**

**Ritual abuse** involves physical, sexual, emotional and psychological abuse of a person. It usually begins in early childhood and frequently carries on into adult life. It often involves multiple abusers, both male and female and multiple victims and is highly organised. Sometimes, the abusers make use of a complex belief system to control their victims and attempt to justify the many acts of abuse they carry out. The abusers frequently claim allegiance to a secretive religion or faith that they follow, which, they claim, fully condones the abusive acts.

This type of abuse often, but not always, begins in the home, in the family setting and often the whole family is involved in maintaining it. When this is the case, much of the early teaching occurs at home so that the children are indoctrinated into it from birth. Often, the religion has been practised within such families for many generations and is passed on through children who are initially forced when young and later, as they grow older, persuaded into it. For some it becomes a way of life that suits them and from which they benefit. This is not the case for all, even when involved from birth.

Survivors of this type of abuse rarely regard what has happened to them as abuse at first and are often so caught up in the belief system that they may believe what the abusers did to them was for their own good. Though they will not have liked the things that happened, they may have been taught that they had to learn how to behave properly. They are often taught that what is happening to them is right and pre-ordained by a higher power. Often the fact that they resist and do not like what is happening is used against them as proof that they are unworthy or inadequate. Often the survivor who escapes from the abuse carries on believing that they were the ones who failed in enduring and cooperating, rather than believing that the people in their lives were abusers and wrong in what they were doing.

Survivors of this type of abuse frequently talk about rape, torture, mind control, use of drugs, hypnotism and murder. They talk about extremes of sensory deprivation, abuse during incredible rituals and abuse continuing at home. They all seem to find it very difficult to break away from the abusers, many of whom are close relatives, and have been so thoroughly silenced by the abusers, that even years later, they often find it almost impossible to talk about what has happened to them. Frequently when they do try to talk they feel extreme physical pain, which gets worse the more they try to talk. Often they believe that the pain is caused by their breach of loyalty and that the abusers know that they are talking.

Children are extensively used and abused within this context and children and adults are often forced to abuse others. Most survivors will talk at some point of witnessing scenes of child murder, mostly of unregistered children or premature babies, and some female survivors will talk of being made deliberately pregnant so that the group can have their child to use during rituals. Such is the unbelievability of some of the barbarous acts described by survivors that many people prefer to believe that such things cannot possibly happen in a civilised society.

## Conspiracy Theories ➤

People involved in secret and abusive groups, societies and religions come from all walks of life and all sorts of backgrounds. On the outside, in the world that most people know, they go about their business like any other person. They appear as normal as anyone else, act as normally as anyone else and they are employed in a wide variety of professions and businesses. They have normal hobbies, normal families, do good deeds and community work as often as anyone else and effectively operate as normally as everyone else in society. To all intents and purposes, they are normal. No one can ever tell just by looking at any one of them that they are involved in ritual abuse.

Abusers such as these usually represent a good cross section of the community. Because these people come from all walks of life and work in many different professions, survivors are frequently extremely afraid of some professionals such as doctors, social workers, teachers and others who might actually be able to help them. Such is their experience of being abused by a variety of individuals, some of whom they know work as professionals, they do not know who they can trust in large agencies and they often fear approaching such agencies for help in case there is an abuser working there.

It is very difficult for people working in agencies such as social services or health, for example, to begin to accept the fears of survivors as many practitioners think of their profession as sacred. Because they are carers of people themselves and could not contemplate being involved in the abuse of another person, they find it hard to believe that anyone in their line of work could do such a thing. On top of this, they cannot contemplate the idea of an abuser ever working in their own field. Many of them expect survivors to trust them simply because they are teachers, social workers or doctors and cannot begin to see the perspective of the survivors.

Many survivors are thought to be paranoid because they fear and distrust everyone, and sometimes think that there is a conspiracy of some kind against them. Yet, when they begin to talk about some of the difficulties faced when they approach some agencies for help, it quickly becomes apparent that there is often some justification behind some of their concerns. Though many of their fears are not actually justified in that not everyone in a particular agency can be involved with abusive groups, sometimes, a worker in an agency is involved and it only takes one person in a key agency to make life difficult for a survivor. The survivors, aware that abusers can actually be working anywhere, have no idea at all whom they can trust and are on their guard all the time, particularly when dealing with larger faceless agencies.

Survivors have often faced extreme difficulty when approaching different agencies. For example, with the Benefits Agencies survivors sometimes have problems in getting benefits in the first place with strange things happening, such as case notes going missing, mistakes being made about their entitlement and letters being sent to the wrong address. In the health service, survivors have experienced missing records, miss-information in their records, lack of response to requests for help as referrals have gone astray, miss-diagnosis of illness and a variety of other problems that have the effect of delaying essential medical treatment. In housing, survivors have encountered similar problems with countless delays, loss of, or wrong information provided about them, information disappearing off the computer system and difficulties even in being able to get access to a home.

While it is relatively easy to put a great deal of the problems encountered by survivors down to their inexperience of dealing with the various systems and some of the systems being inefficient in the extreme, many survivors experience repeated problems every single time they interact with some of these agencies. Surprisingly, or not, depending on how you think, as soon as someone else, especially another agency, starts to query what is going on, all the problems quickly smooth out, until the next time the survivor contacts the agency.

The most common thing you hear in response to queries regarding the latest problem that a survivor relates about benefits, housing or health is, 'I've never heard of anything like that before!' Or, 'that just cannot happen!' Again and again survivors are faced with almost unbelievable problems in relation to getting access to some of the services that most other people take for granted. Faced with this, any worker supporting the survivor often begins to wonder themselves who in the agency concerned is deliberately messing things up for the survivor, and why. It happens so consistently that it becomes easy to believe that there is indeed a deliberate conspiracy being carried out against the survivor, by one or more people working within the agency concerned. Often, for the survivor who is trying to escape from the abusive situation, the bottom line is that they have no money, housing or health care for such a long period of time that they sometimes have no choices left open to them and have to go back to the abusers in order to survive.

Whether or not there is actually a conspiracy against individual survivors masterminded by the group they have left, or there is one individual in the agency that is making many deliberate mistakes, or these agencies are consistently and completely incompetent when it comes to dealing with ritual abuse survivors, is debatable. Unfortunately, survivors often become so used to it, that they accept as a fact that any of their dealings with particular agencies, will always lead to real difficulties for them. No one ever investigates what is really going on, as any complaints are always dealt with internally in most agencies. There are never any answers given as to why these things are able to happen, continually, to one individual.

One small example of this happened to a homeless survivor who filled in all the forms at the housing department. One week later, on returning to the same housing department, no record existed of these forms. The forms were filled in again. Another week later, the housing department again could not find them. Once again the forms were completed this time with a witness present. Four weeks later an offer of a house was made. On going to see the house with the housing officer, the house was seen to be in a major state of disrepair. It turned out that the house offer was a mistake and the offer was withdrawn. This same mistake was repeated twice more over the course of the next few weeks. Soon after the third house was offered and subsequently declared by the housing officer to be unfit to offer, the survivor received a letter telling her that as three offers of a house had been made and refused, she was no longer considered to be homeless.

The survivor had to go back again to the housing department and complete forms again as the case had been closed. The next catalogue of errors then began with the wrong details being found on computer, rent arrears suddenly showing up which were inaccurate and offers of the wrong sized house. All this continued for nearly a year before finally the survivor enlisted the aid of a local councillor. At this point all errors ceased and a house was finally provided. It is easy to see with this type of example, which incidentally was echoed twice more with the same survivor some years later and resulted in even greater farces, how a survivor can begin to believe that someone in a particular department or agency might have it in for them and be deliberately causing them trouble. In this case, luckily, the survivor had people to turn to for help. Some survivors, who had found themselves in this position, would be forced to return to the abusers, as they would quite simply have nowhere else to go.

While many of us can tell of silly mistakes being made by some agencies, few people ever encounter the multitude of problems that are consistently experienced by ritual abuse survivors in relation to these same agencies. The other thing that seems to happen consistently is the leaking of personal information. Some survivors, who have succeeded in escaping the abuse and have remained hidden from the abusers for a long time, suddenly find that the abusers track them down. The amazing coincidence that goes with this is the fact that the survivor has recently contacted an agency such as social services, benefits agency, housing or medical centres for the first time ever. Survivors are not very trusting and may not be justified in believing that some sort of a conspiracy exists against them, but in view of some of the difficulties they often experience, it is easy to see how they might begin to believe as they do.

Chapter 4

Group
Mechanics

Chapter 4
**Group Mechanics**

**There are many types and kinds of secretive groups that exist in the world,** some of which are not abusive in nature but follow a similar belief system to the abusive groups, to a point. For example Hermetic orders are groups who all follow a similar belief system with minor differences in some beliefs and practices of the groups. These groups all have a similar theme of 'do what thou wilt shall be the whole of the law' though some of them do add on 'providing it does no harm' to the statement. There are Masonic groups, which are sometimes linked or affiliated to the Thelemic orders. Within some groups there are often different sub-groups and levels, such as the Golden Dawn, Red Rose and Astrum Argentium or Silver Star through which people involved can progress depending on their individual learning and degree of skill.

Many survivors of ritual abuse will talk about their abusive groups being affiliated to orders such as the Thelemic order or the Masonic order and of their group following similar beliefs and practices to these orders. Whether it is actually true that abusive groups are in reality affiliated to these orders or not, is difficult to tell, but it is certainly often the belief of some survivors that they are. Similarly, survivors of some cults believe that their group was affiliated to Christian orders such as Catholics, Jehovah's Witnesses or Mormons.

There is a great deal of information available, particularly on the Internet about the lesser-known religions. An example of one of the more secretive religions is Thelema. Followers of Thelemic orders generally have similar beliefs. Thelema is a Greek word meaning will or intention. The basic belief is that people should attempt to find out what their True Will is, and do it, while not interfering with the True Will of others. Followers generally believe that there is no right and wrong interpretation of Thelema and people should work things out for themselves. In this way, it is believed that each person will gain personal freedom.

Although, various Thelemic orders can be traced back many centuries, in 1904, it was revived by the writings and teachings of Alistair Crowley (1875-1947), who became its new prophet. He was then known as Master Therion. Crowley became a member of the Golden Dawn in 1898 and after travelling, studying and then writing several books declared that the New Aeon of Horus had began on the 20th March 1904. Crowley subsequently, in 1925, became head of the Ordo Templi Orientis (O.T.O) in Germany, which was at one time a Freemason's group. He gave this order a new mission, which was to spread the word of Thelema.

Crowley was hugely influential in shaping the thinking and practices of many of the more secretive groups. Groups which follow Thelema generally celebrate the 20th March as the new year, the 3 days of writing (Crowley's book) on 8th, 9th and 10th April, 12th August (Prophet and his bride day), October 12th as Crowleymas (Crowley's birth date) and the 1st of December as Crowley's Greater Feast (date of his death). In addition to these dates, followers usually celebrate the Equinoxes and Solstices.

Genuine followers of Thelema, as with most other religions, are absolutely forbidden by their religion to abuse anyone. Yet, abusers do not generally follow anyone's rules and can twist the words and practices of any religion to suit their own ends. Because of this, survivors can sometimes assume that the whole religion and all involved in it, are corrupt, when in fact, it has only been their own group of abusers who have twisted that particular religion.

Many survivors, particularly those who are Satanic abuse survivors, are deeply afraid of secretive religions such as Thelemic orders or Masonic orders because they have been taught that it is the religion which is abusive and therefore they often think that all followers must be the same. While a survivor's experience is valid for them in terms of their own experience of a religious group, it does not necessarily follow that all people who follow a secretive religion are abusive. Neither does it mean that the religion is corrupt or abusive. What it means is that abusers can and do twist things to suit themselves and survivors believe what they have lived and experienced.

Piecing together what survivors say about the groups can be difficult, as survivors have their own individual experiences and different perspectives on it and come from a variety of independent groups. Having said that, by listening to survivors, a structural pattern of the groups begins to emerge, one, which is fairly consistent across individuals and their groups.

Each group usually has autonomy and is hierarchical in structure. Above each group, there is a higher group, or inner circle, sometimes consisting of the top people from several groups. Individuals can aspire to and join this higher group if they become skilled enough. Above the inner circle is another layer of the same.  This tiered pattern continues until participation is strictly by invitation and ability. There are some groups that seem to recruit individuals by invitation only and the higher up the group, the more selective and secretive it becomes. Somewhere at the top of it all, many survivors believe, there are groups such as the Illuminati.

This group of people are reputed to believe that they are to be the chosen few who will through intrigue, murder and manipulation eventually rule the world and its masses. This group of people believe they have the right to rule mainly because they believe themselves to be more ruthless, powerful and intelligent than other people. Many survivors also believe them to be the people at the top of the pornography, drugs and arms industries.

There are also other types of group spoken about by survivors, such as santerians, setians, pagans, druids and witches. Again, it is important to point out that there are many people who follow these ancient faiths and do not act abusively towards others. These people are harmlessly following old religions and would never dream of harming or abusing anyone. In fact, many of them would argue that their faith dictates that they must do no harm to others. It has to be said though, that some survivors talk about being within groups such as these, which were very abusive. They talk about covens of witches who practise black magic, druids meetings where children are sacrificed and pagan ceremonies where the most horrendous abuse goes on during the ceremonies.

In addition to this, some survivors talk about groups, which claim to be Christian yet again turning the religion round to act abusively to the children and adult survivors in their power. The reality is that no matter which faith is claimed by the abusers, they are perfectly able and willing to turn it round to their own ends and use it in a destructive way against those people they hold power over. You only have to think of the many atrocities carried out throughout the world in the name of one religion or another, despite that religion stating such things as killing is wrong, to  understand how people can turn any system of faith into a means of overpowering and abusing whole nations, groups of people and individuals.

## Rituals➢

People, except for survivors, generally use the word 'ritual' quite liberally when talking about ritual abuse but as survivors are usually reluctant to go into any specific detail about what this actually means, many people are left with a very vague sense of what occurs. To begin to try and understand some of the things that go on during rituals, it is easiest to begin by thinking of an established and acceptable religion such as Catholicism.

In this faith, during worship, depending on what type of service is occurring, the priest and others involved in the service dress in a particular, often highly ornate style. They wear robes of different colours, depending on their status and the ceremony being performed. There are often candles burning in the room or being lit at particular times, set things that are being said or chanted, set responses expected from the congregation, readings from a Bible, songs, chants and prayers. Around the room, there are particular symbolic elements such as crosses, statues, paintings or other symbols representing Christ and other artefacts of importance to the faith. There is also usually an altar, which can often be the focus of events.

Many different religions of the world have their own particular trappings, symbols, language and set routines or rituals that they carry out at regular and prescribed times, places and in a particularly revered manner. They have their hierarchy, ordained ministers of the faith and followers or worshippers. They employ methods of teaching the faith to the children from a relatively young age and often have particular levels of attainment, initiation and acceptance into the faith. These things are part of the worship and reverence of the people involved in the faith and as such are extremely important and powerful to them. These religions are mostly harmless to people and for many, help them live a fulfilled and meaningful life.

Secret religions and groups that survivors talk about, often behave in exactly the same manner as these legitimate churches, to a point. All of the things described in catholic worship and other religions are done to some degree in cults and satanic worship. The big difference is that some of the secret religions are extremely abusive of some people during the worship, they are praying to a different god and the rituals are designed to control and terrify their victims. Many of the abusers claim to be believers in their faith and intent on worshipping their own deity in their own way, but groups which incorporate abuse as part of their worship will not do so openly as to do so, would, quite rightly, lead to instant prosecution in this and most other countries of the world.

Because the activities carried out during such things as abusive satanic rituals are illegal, the places used are varied. The groups very carefully choose the places they intend to meet in and then prepare the place for the rituals, which are to be performed. Often the floor area to be used is covered with a large sheet of tarpaulin. If a large area is to be used, they will provide several sheets of tarpaulin. The tarpaulin usually has the symbols used by the group painted or printed on it, and its main purpose is to prevent any evidence of the abuse from being left behind. Most groups have a tarpaulin, which is kept specifically for this purpose and it is often stored in places such as farm buildings or warehouses where it would not be seen to be out of place. Some of the tarpaulins are old and have been in the 'family' for many years. Others, due to the rapid destruction of their heirloom if anyone starts to look too closely at any of the group members, are modern lighter versions.

Before, and more frequently during, the rituals, symbols may be drawn in blood or other body fluids on the tarpaulin, on the walls or onto some individuals. The blood is sometimes animal blood but more frequently, depending on the type of group, the particular event and the beliefs, it is often human blood taken either willingly or unwillingly from an individual in the group.

In addition to the tarpaulin, associated group symbols are drawn or hung on the walls, candles are set out at various points in the space being used and an altar is set up. This altar is sometimes made by the abusers, making use of something that is already present such as a gravestone, table or other flat surface or it may be made out of something brought in by the group. Either way, the altar is frequently person sized and sometimes initially covered by an ornate altar cloth. Sometimes the various items to be used during the ceremony (knife, dagger, chalice, bowls, etc) are placed carefully on this altar. Often they are covered or wrapped in cloth or skin until the rituals begin.

From the perspective of most survivors, they are not usually involved in these particular preparations, unless they are being trained to perform rituals. Instead, for weeks before the ceremony, any survivors who have to take part are being prepared for what is to happen during the ritual. This, in reality, means that the abusers often take the survivor through their part in the proceedings to come over and over again until they are certain that the survivor will perform their part properly. This usually involves taking part in forced sexual activity of some kind, responding to the abusers demands in a multitude of different ways, both physical and sexual violence, and behaving exactly in the way that the abusers have decreed they must.

Survivors may only know which role they themselves have to play in the forthcoming event. They may not know the finer detail of what is to actually occur. They are often completely unaware of the other things that will happen, particularly to others, until the events actually begin to happen. This means that many occurrences can be very frightening and confusing and survivors are often witness to, and sometimes part of, some horrendous acts of abuse. A simple example of this might be a survivor who knows that they will be tied on an inverted cross to be sexually and physically abused by others. However, during the event another person is tied to the survivor linking them together in such a way that any movement by one causes hurt to the other. The abusers then make certain that lack of movement is impossible by forcing one person or the other to move thus causing severe pain to the other person. This can have the effect of setting survivor against survivor as the will to survive can, with some people, rapidly overtake any caring about other individuals.

Often, the events organised by groups last for several days, and on some occasions for weeks. Not all survivors will take part in the whole ceremony. Some will be kept incarcerated nearby until the group reaches the parts of the proceedings that involves them. Children to be used are sometimes kept subdued by drugs or by an older survivor who is put in charge of them and ordered to keep them quiet. Any unwelcome noise leads to the severe punishment of the child survivor and the older survivor in charge. Often this older survivor is still a child. In an attempt to lessen the overall suffering, survivors are often placed in the position of going to extremes to try and keep hysterical and terrified young children quiet.

All survivors report that they are thoroughly cleaned and scrubbed before entering the proceedings and even the cleansing is very abusive and intrusive. Sometimes very hot or very cold water is used, survivors are completely immersed or hosed down and they may be roughly scrubbed with a rough brush or other such object. Often the cleaning includes inner cleansing such as making sure that the stomach and bowels are empty. The survivor may be told that this cleansing is essential so that their impurities do not tarnish the ritual, but it is probably more to do with making sure that survivors are not able to vomit etc, during the ritual. Bodily hair may be shaved off and sometimes, depending on the event; oil or other substances are rubbed over all or parts of the body. This cleansing routine may be repeated several times during the ritual.

Sometimes, at the beginning of the event, the survivor is dressed in a robe. Nothing is worn underneath. Survivors report the abusers' reading from the group 'Bible', chanting, swaying and dancing themselves into frenzy. Often, the participants of the event, i.e. the abusers, stand in a close semi-circle round the altar and often survivors talk about being placed on the altar where they are then abused, firstly by those people who are officiating, and then by all group members. Survivors also talk about being kept tied or chained to items such as hooks, crosses or the altar for long periods of time and periodically being abused during different parts of the ritual.

Survivors talk about the different colours worn by abusers and survivors to indicate their status. Through the colours worn, everyone knows at a glance which position is held and where everyone is in the pecking order. This also applies to the children. Generally speaking, there are two types of people, those who hold power and position or who will come into a position of power and those who will never be allowed any power or status. The second group of people are those who are considered the 'expendable property' of the group and are considered to be there to be used and abused by all present. Practically anything is allowed to be done to these people and children are actively encouraged to abuse them.

The other thing that it is common for survivors to talk about is the use of young children. While all children suffer similar abuse while very young and are often made to abuse one another, some of those children are destined to gain a position of power in the group and are soon regarded as 'privileged' compared to other children. This so-called 'privilege' means that sometimes these children are made to torture and abuse others, and they become as hated and feared by the less 'privileged' children as the adult abusers. The least 'privileged' children can feel completely betrayed by those children who were once the same as them but then go on to gain the power to abuse them. In this way, children learn quite young to hate and fear each other and the likelihood of them backing one another up in disclosing the abuse is greatly reduced. Often siblings are deliberately divided in this way to break down any bonds between them.

There is a large difference apparent in any group ritual between those with the power, who are there to enjoy themselves in their so-called worship, and those other people without any power who become the objects to be used and abused by the group. Though all may belong to the same group, equality simply does not exist in this kind of setting. Some people are members because they have chosen to be, other people belong because the group has chosen it to be that way for them and they have no choice in this.

Most of the children and some of the adults are regarded as belonging to the group, in that the group can use them in whatever way they want. These people have no say, no right to an opinion and no power. It is their suffering and pain, which the group would claim provides the energy and the power during rituals. Others within the group have varying degrees of power, depending on their status, but this would not prevent those higher up deciding that they might have to suffer for a while. This is particularly the case if it is thought that anyone is getting above their station or has betrayed the group. It is also a useful way of keeping people in their relevant positions. Those with a little power sometimes become so afraid of being cast back down among the lower orders that they become enthusiastic about what they do to those considered less worthy.

During rituals, some groups, in addition to worshipping their particular god, carry out rituals designed to curse others or raise demons or even the devil himself. These rituals can be very frightening. There are often many minor and major demons that these people, or at least the ones who practise the magic amongst them, believe in and believe they can raise and control. Major demons such as Astarte the goddess of lust and sexuality will be conjured up through using the blood of a child. In reality they may name a group member Astarte, chant weird words, drink a child's blood and claim that the member is now possessed by the spirit of Astarte. This member will then be expected to behave with insatiable lust.

Similarly, the demon Nebiros who is supposed to have the power to inflict harm on others and predict the future will appear on command, usually in the shape of a 'possessed' group member. Baal is raised through a child sacrifice and the demon Moloch is traditionally the destroyer of children.

Though many survivors claim to have witnessed these 'other world' creatures appearing out of Hell on the command of some group members, extremes of fear and pain, dissociation and mind-altering drugs probably help them to appear. Groups also 'persuade' some people that they have been possessed or are in fact representatives of these and other demons. The group, to assist the belief in these creatures, will give some survivors the names of the demons. Despite my scepticism, many survivors and group members believe these things to exist and be possible.

## Betrayal ≻

Any betrayal of the group is ultimately punishable by death. The ultimate betrayal is to tell an outsider about the group or any of its activities. Survivors who have escaped are well aware of this and many will have seen what happens to someone who the group has claimed betrayed them. While this is often a set up arranged to teach a child absolute obedience and eternal silence, with an 'expendable' person chosen to be slowly tortured and killed, all survivors know that telling is a betrayal. Any person accused of betraying the group will be named a traitor and killed during one of the rituals. The symbol used by the group to indicate a traitor will be in evidence round the room and often carved or burned into the skin of the victim as a prelude to the event. A straightforward killing, as in some sacrifices, would not happen. Rather, the abusers would provide for a very long and painful death. This is done to serve as a warning to any others who might consider betrayal.

No one in a group is above the law of betrayal. Regardless of position, any group member who has betrayed the group will be immediately stripped of their position and status. Their change of status will begin immediately upon discovery of their crime. Those at the top, on becoming aware of the crime, will convene a secret meeting to judge the accused. The accused has no right to representation or right to an opinion in this matter. The verdict from this secret meeting will determine the fate of the individual. Immediately after the meeting, the date of punishment will be set and everyone will quickly know that the accused has been deemed guilty. Already they will be set apart from everyone else, no one will be allowed to talk to him or her or try to help them or they will suffer the same fate, and they will be secured in a place from which escape is almost impossible.

Sentence is usually carried out as soon as possible though the abusers will usually look for a particular date to hang it onto. On arrival at the specific place, all will know the sentence. Symbols will adorn the room, specific equipment will be in evidence (used only for such events), and the guilty person will be dressed in **grey** and will already have been the victim of repeated torture. The charges and the sentence will be read out in a ritualised manner and the proceedings will begin. Some groups take great pride in how long they can prolong the suffering of this individual and death is the end result.

The crime of the individual is usually attempting to leave the group or trying to tell an outsider about the group. Whether or not they have actually done this is immaterial if they are of the lower orders as the whole procedure serves as a useful lesson to silence survivors.

Accusing someone who has a higher position is not as easy and many groups, if they think that there has been a betrayal, will bring in people from higher status groups outside their own. If the person, no matter their status, has actually betrayed the group, the end result will be the same as for lower orders. The need to maintain secrecy within these groups is absolute and no one is, or can ever be, above this law. To betray one group is to betray all groups.

Survivors may be condemned in their absence. If for example a survivor has escaped from the group, a meeting will be convened. Sometimes, the group decides that the survivor will remain silent as they consider them to be well enough trained not to talk. In this case, it may suit the group to leave the survivor alone and just pull them back in from time to time to reinforce the training. In other cases, it is decided that the survivor is a traitor and a death sentence is imposed. The fact that sometimes the survivor is safeguarded from the group is immaterial. What it means is, if the abusers ever regain control of the survivor, they will kill them. When the abusers are consistently unable to get to the survivor, they will tell the lower members and survivors in the group that they have killed the traitor. Survivors remaining in the group have no way of knowing whether or not this is true unless they ever see the so-called traitor alive and well.

Survivors who escape are a great embarrassment to a group. For a start it lets other survivors know that escape is actually possible. Also, given that groups are claiming to be allied to a higher power, which can do anything and is claimed to provide the group with huge power, a powerless survivor just walking away from the group shows this to be the nonsense that it is. Groups try to get round this internally by claiming such things as, the survivor is dead, the survivor is working for them or that they cast the person out of the group. All these lies are intended to cover the fact that a survivor escaped and they have no real power except over those they hold captive.

It is little wonder though, that survivors who escape are terrified of being found and often return to the group of their own accord time and time again. Even those who eventually manage to get away remain very afraid that the group will catch up with them. Many survivors continue to maintain the silence years afterwards, as they are far too afraid to 'betray' the group by talking. Most survivors have seen for themselves the cost of betrayal and few would be willing to risk the consequences.

Survivors rarely talk about the sexual abuse that happens as being the worst part of the abuse. When they can reach the stage of talking, they are much more likely to describe events such as witnessing child murder, being shut in a box and buried for a long period of time, being repeatedly taken to the point of death, believing they are about to die, extremes of sensory deprivation, electric shocks or being forced to be pregnant and their child being killed before them. Some even talk about being forced to kill the child themselves. It is very often the mental and emotional torture that survivors have endured that is more relevant to them than any kind of rape or sexual violence.

Most survivors will not talk at all about the actual rituals they have been involved in. They may eventually talk about some of the abuses that they endured but few will break silence about the worship. For many it is because survivors know that this, if the group discovered it, would be the ultimate crime against all groups. Others, because they still hold to the belief system they grew up with, would see it as betraying the deity and their fear of retribution prevents them from talking. Some are just so conditioned that they cannot actually talk about it and any attempt to do so causes them too much pain to endure. They therefore avoid talking. Though it is rare for survivors to talk about the rituals, some survivors do get to a stage where they can do so. It is only when they get to this stage and actually start talking that they realise that the group and the deity the group worships is, in reality, powerless to stop them from talking to anyone about any aspect of their experience.

Chapter 5

# Beliefs
# and Faith

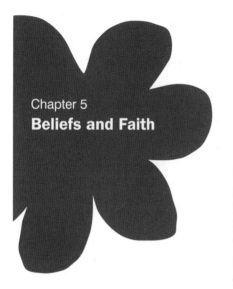

Chapter 5
## Beliefs and Faith

**Many survivors of ritual abuse grow up with a faith that they still firmly believe in, even after they have finally escaped from the group.** Though this faith may be at odds and in many cases, completely opposite to the prevailing faith of the culture they are living in, it is no less powerful to the survivor. In this country, although Christianity is currently the majority faith, it is by no means the only religion being believed in and practised by people. Generally speaking, Britain is tolerant of other faiths and the freedom to worship and belong to any faith or religion is part and parcel of the rights of any member of this society. The European Convention on Human Rights provides for the freedom to follow the religion of your choice.

Just as there can exist a deeply held belief in the existence of God and/or Christ, despite the absence of any concrete evidence as to their existence, so too there can be a deeply held belief in the existence of Satan and a variety of demons from Hell. Indeed some Christians and some other faiths do believe in the existence of an opposing deity. For many who experience and survive ritual abuse, the existence of

Satan will have been 'proven' to them on many occasions. If someone is repeatedly hurting you and telling you that they are doing this in the name of Satan or some other deity, then this is your experience and there is little choice but to believe it.

Most survivors will have seen and heard evidence of his existence. That this experience is presented through the constant use of hypnosis, use of mind-altering drugs and extremes of torture and mind control, does not in any way alter the experiences of the survivor. They, like everyone else, believe that what they have experienced at first hand is real. It is certainly real to them. Even when they can later work out some of the tricks used to make them see and hear things that were not there, they cannot deny the reality of their own senses. In the same way that some people can believe that they have seen or communicated directly with God, so too can survivors believe they have seen or communicated with Satan. This type of experience is subjective to the individual concerned and no one has the right to say that it cannot have happened.

Survivors escaping from the group often carry their beliefs in the faith of the group with them. This does not mean that they necessarily agree with what the abusers do, most do not. Many do however, believe that the abuse inflicted on them was right and proper and was part of their destiny but can see that the abuse inflicted by the group on others, particularly the children was wrong. Many believe that if they talk, the group will know about it and punish them for it. Other beliefs may include such things as; they have no rights, their soul is owned by or 'tied' to the devil, they cannot enter a Christian church, they are evil or they will make the people around them turn bad. While many of these beliefs can be damaging to survivors, sometimes all they have left is their beliefs and it may be more damaging to try and deny the beliefs of survivors. In time, people can challenge their own beliefs and come to reject some of the more damaging beliefs for themselves.

While there is no problem in accepting that people have the right to follow any faith they choose, Satanism is not commonly regarded as a popular or acceptable faith to follow in this country. The very word causes people to automatically think of abuse, abnormal practices and evil. For this reason, few would admit openly to practising it. Those few, who would admit it, will always claim that no children are involved in it and that no abuse ever takes place in the name of their faith. This may well be the case for some.

Adult survivors of satanic abuse however talk of murder, torture, mutilation, sacrifice of animals and people, rape and a multitude of abuses carried out in the name of the group worshipping Satan. Many survivors grow up in the religious faith of their abusers and though they may escape from the abuse, may still hold onto the belief system. This makes it very difficult for them to come to terms with their abuse and extremely difficult for supporters who hold a different belief system to the survivor to understand.

Satanism teaches that people should follow their own will rather than the will of a weak god or society in general. It teaches that personal gain, indulgence and personal gratification is right and that to be powerful is everything. Survival of the fittest and the right of the strongest to rule over those who are weaker is a key element. Satanists generally view mankind as just another animal but the most vicious animal  of all. Though mankind can think and reason, this to some only means that we are clever animals. Written in the Satanic Bible amongst the nine satanic statements are:

❶   Satan represents indulgence instead of abstinence!

❷   Satan represents vital existence instead of spiritual pipe dreams!

*The first of the nine satanic sins is stated as 'stupidity-*
*the cardinal sin of Satanism'.*
*The fifth sin is herd conformity ie blindly following the beliefs*
*of others*

Many Satanists would claim that mankind has been duped and controlled by a weak god designed by man, which prohibits everything that people are naturally designed to enjoy. They would claim that belief in a god is simply a way of controlling the masses and only stupid people would follow this path. They might also declare that as people have free will, they should naturally follow their own paths in life and think for themselves. The natural path of mankind, they would argue, is towards survival of the fittest and doing anything that is enjoyable and natural. With abusive groups they would argue that their power is part of the natural order and they have the right to do with others, who are less fit and powerful than them, as they please. Obviously, there are many who would disagree with them.

Although people do have the right to follow and practise the religion of their choice, with rights should always come the responsibility to consider the rights of others. Followers of abusive satanic groups do have the right to believe in what they want to but they do not have the right to force their beliefs on other people or the right to deny rights to others. Survivors of ritual abuse do have the right to believe in whatever they wish as do their abusers, but no one ever has the right to abuse another person or living creature or deny any of the rights of others.

## Why is it so hard to accept or believe? ➤

It is incredibly hard for many people to accept or believe that ritual abuse happens because to do so would be tantamount to accepting the unacceptable and believing in the unbelievable. To believe that ritual abuse actually happens also means the complete destruction of a person's world view which can result in extreme inner conflict as the mind struggles to make sense of a completely different and opposing reality to what the person believes really goes on in the world.

In order to accept that ritual abuse may be going on, especially in your own community, you first have to be able to accept that people, maybe even people you know, are capable of atrocious acts of depravity, rape, torture, sadism and even child murder. Many people shield themselves from the unacceptability of all this through denial of the possibility that anyone could ever be capable of doing such terrible things. To come to believe that seemingly normal people are capable of such atrocities can so alter a person's world view that they are often rendered helpless and deeply shocked. Often the mind simply cannot cope with such an upheaval in beliefs. Their belief in a safe and ordered world in which people care for one another and the children in particular, begins to fragment and many people take refuge in complete denial. To begin to change this denial takes time.

Denial of the existence of ritual abuse is common and can be a way of protecting one's self from becoming completely overwhelmed by the unacceptable reality of such abuse happening. Even survivors and supporters of survivors take refuge in denial from time to time despite, or even because of, their own experiences. Denial is the minds first line of defence and is a completely normal human coping mechanism which all of us experience when we are faced with something that we just cannot come to terms with in our lives.

It is very difficult to get concrete evidence about ritual abuse. Firstly, ritual abuse is not a recognised crime in many countries. The abuse that occurs within it is usually a criminal offence but the addition of almost unbelievable rituals, makes the whole experience sound fantastic and thereby, almost impossible for survivors to tell and for outsiders to hear. For certain, the easiest way to abuse a child and then get away with it is to dress up in robes, behave strangely, dance round a fire, chant and wear a weird mask. Then if the child tries to describe these events or tell about their experience, no one will be able to believe them. Even believing that a child has been abused or raped is hard enough for most people to take on, but if the additional factors such as carrying out weird rituals are added to the equation, it simply becomes far too much for most people to take on and believe.

Also, if there is no actual crime of ritual abuse to address, there can never be any real and sustained search for any evidence of it. No one will ever take the time to look for evidence of a crime that simply does not exist. Criminals, unless they are of the extremely stupid variety, seldom leave the evidence of their crimes lying about waiting to be discovered by the police. Normally once a crime of any kind is committed and subsequently reported, the police begin to search for the evidence that will indicate who did it, how they did it and how the perpetrators can be caught and brought to justice. With ritual abuse no one can report it as a crime in its own right and no one will therefore look for any real evidence that it ever happened. Why would anyone ever commit resources to seeking something that is not a recorded crime and they do not believe exists in the first place?

Survivors are extremely well conditioned not to talk. This conditioning usually begins at a very early age and continues throughout the period of abuse. It is relatively easy for any adult to make a child believe anything that they say. Children have nothing to compare their beliefs and adults' statements with and have little choice but to believe what they have been taught. They can, therefore, end up in the position of repeating things that everyone knows just cannot be true i.e. a statement such as, 'Santa and his reindeer hurt my bum.' Santa is a mythical figure therefore this simply cannot be true. Reindeer are not the usual kind of creatures to be found hanging about in Scotland, therefore this part of the statement is very unlikely. Yet, the child may have been told that one of the persons hurting them was Santa and the objects used to hurt the child may have been called reindeer by the abusers. How would the child know any differently? A child making such a fantastic statement would be very unlikely to be believed by anyone, yet from the child's perspective the statement may be true for him or her.

It is very rare for a ritual abuse survivor to initiate any contact with the police or any other statutory agency. Not only are they conditioned not to tell, but also adult survivors know that they will just not be believed if they try to disclose. Survivors know and have been taught that to talk to the police is the ultimate betrayal and that, not only will they suffer, but also others left behind in the group, will suffer the consequences of such a betrayal. This will have been proven to them many times before. The real experience of survivors, which is the only thing they will have to go on, will be that any threats by group members are not idle threats. Few, if any, survivors ever reach adulthood without witnessing what happens to those who are deemed to have betrayed the family and the group. All of this makes it unlikely that survivors will talk to the police.

In childhood, survivors will have been told that to talk to outsiders will result in extremes of torture and ultimate death. They will have witnessed the fact that these threats can and will be carried out. Most child and adult survivors, when they can eventually talk, will recount having seen murders and mutilations carried out. Most survivors will talk about being punished in an extreme manner for trying to talk when young. It is for this reason that it is usually several years before survivors who have finally reached safety begin to talk. Such is the enforced secrecy, that even when they do begin the painful process of disclosing the abuse, every time they tell a little bit, they become completely overwhelmed by fear and anxiety for days or even weeks afterwards. All survivors share the same reluctance to disclose, and the more horrendous the experience, the more unwilling or unable they become to talk about it. All survivors fear the consequences of talking both in terms of what the group will do to them for talking and because they justifiably fear the disbelief of the person they try to talk to.

When survivors, especially child survivors, talk about their experiences, there is often a high degree of incredible and impossible events disclosed. This serves to further discredit the survivors. Consider the survivor who talks about having witnessed a murder and then having seen the murder victim brought back to life. That the survivor relating such an impossible event can really believe what they have seen is irrefutable, but there is no way that this type of event could really have happened. When this sort of event is thrown into the equation, the whole story that is being told by the survivor is thrown into doubt. Yet it is relatively easy to deceive a child or even an adult who is experiencing extreme abuse. Abusers can and do deliberately trick and deceive their victims to increase their hold over them, make the survivor believe that the abusers actually have power over life and death, and to ensure that if the survivor ever gets away and tries to talk to anyone, no one will ever believe what they say.

Another factor, which can discredit survivors of ritual abuse, is round the issue of evidence. A survivor can relate such things as having witnessed a murder and seeing the bodies being buried in a particular place, but on going back to that place, no bodies are found there. The survivor can only relate their own direct experience of what they witnessed and may well be telling the truth as far as they know it. Unfortunately, abusers who rely on secrecy to continue what they are doing are not stupid. Yes, there may well have been a murder followed by a burial, but it would be sheer stupidity if the abusers left a corpse in a place that a child or adult survivor capable of getting away from the group might later identify. Common practice in abusive groups is to remove all evidence of their crimes including what is left of any bodies. The survivor would never be privy to this information and the only ones with the knowledge of what happens to evidence would be those who are well established and high up members of the group.

Satanism and other abusive cult practices are not a new phenomenon, as is often declared by those who argue that it does not exist in modern times. It is not something that only appeared out of the blue in the 1990's. For a start, survivors were talking to supporters in rape crisis centres long before the 1990's. Any researcher into history, both recent and ancient, can uncover documented accounts of demonic worship, torture, child rape, child sacrifice and ritualised abuse. There is even mention of Satanism in the Bible. Human nature is a constant over thousands of years and although modern people would prefer to believe that we are now so civilised that we are all beyond committing such acts of cruelty upon a child, this is simply not the case. Every newspaper daily carries details of adults raped as children, child murder and child torture. The Internet circulates thousands of images of extreme brutality towards children to people who enjoy and get sexual pleasure from seeing these images of children suffering. Those children used to make the hard-core pornography and snuff movies that are in circulation on the Internet, had to come from somewhere.

Every generation throws up individuals who will seek to have power and control over others and be prepared to fly in the face of law and cultural norms in order to pursue their own ends. Power hungry individuals who have broken through, or care nothing for, cultural prohibitions will do anything to satisfy  their own needs at the expense of others. Such individuals will stop at nothing to satisfy their own gratification and insatiable quest for more power.

Even in recent history there are many examples of people who are more than capable of unimaginable atrocities and also capable of swaying huge numbers of people to accept and embrace whatever philosophy, religion or belief they advocate. Possibly the best example of this was Hitler and the rise of Nazism. This is also a good example of elitism, getting rid of evidence, persuading people to collude and the range of atrocities that people are actually capable of when they follow a particular set of beliefs. Abusive groups can behave in very much the same way as the Nazi regime albeit on a much smaller scale.

Few people want to believe that ritual abuse is a reality for anyone living in this country, and probably all of us would rather it was either a very rare occurrence or did not exist. If we are ever to uncover the real truth about what goes on though, we must be ready and willing to believe and hear all available information from all different perspectives, regardless of our own worldview and beliefs. We must also be willing to look for the evidence. The abusers are never going to tell us anything so we must stay open to listening to the survivors. The people who are most likely to believe that ritual abuse is practised in our society are still the people who have come into contact with survivors.

Chapter 6

# Meeting Places

Chapter 6
## Meeting Places

**Groups, because of their abusive practices are, of necessity, highly secretive and will go to great lengths to ensure that no one on the outside can find out about them.** Though for centuries they have maintained a tradition in what they do and how they do it, some of their practices have had to change with the times. In the past, they would more often meet in the open air to carry out many of their rituals. The places chosen in the past were always isolated and were often in a traditional setting such as an old castle, beside standing stones or no longer used graveyard. Despite the relative safety of isolation, groups would still always safeguard themselves from discovery by setting up a system of security guards surrounding the chosen site to ensure that no one could stumble across them. Although groups might use the same place more than once, they would rarely do so in any regular order and would tend to vary, at random, the places they met.

Some of the reasons for the change in meeting places are, the increase in the general population in the country and peoples' increasing mobility into more remote areas. Fewer places are now inaccessible to everyone and fewer places are strictly private. As a result of this, less young survivors report as many open-air activities as older survivors do. This seems to be the main difference between the experiences of older and younger survivors.

Obviously, abusers meeting in one another's homes to carry out their abusive practices leads to maximum security and many do this and have always done this on a regular basis. Many ordinary houses have attics and basements, which can be easily converted and used by small groups of people. However, group members with larger houses are often deliberately recruited and are expected to accommodate and host the meetings more often than those from council estates. Having said that, even within ordinary homes, a great deal of abuse and ritual activity can and does take place. Abusers, particularly those with high position in the group, often make quite a lot of money from the group activities and this enables them to buy or rent property, which is secluded or secure enough to be used.

Due to the fear of discovery, open-air activities now tend to be rare in this country except in the very remote places such as the Highlands and Islands. Instead, greater use is now made of large buildings such as barns, church halls, factories and warehouses. Sometimes groups access these places because amongst their membership people own  or can get free access to them, other times the groups simply hire their venues for a period of time. Many large places are available to rent and the group is hardly likely to state the real purpose behind the booking of any venue.

It is quite rare for groups to have a permanent set up these days because if this were ever discovered, questions would be asked which might be difficult to answer and abusers would not want to draw attention to themselves or leave any proof lying about. Having said this, the trappings of such abuse would not always be readily recognised by most ordinary people. A large stone slab in the centre of a field or barn would not be recognised by most people as representing an altar, though it might be used as one by a group. Metal rings set in the stone walls of a barn can be for tying up cattle and horses, or used to tie or chain survivors. Wooden and metal frames and cages can be for containing livestock and this can easily be extended to using these items for abusing survivors. Abusers are very adaptable and are rarely stupid people. Items, which may be out of place in one setting, are perfectly ordinary in another and the abusers are very careful to keep everything looking as normal as possible. They would not, for example have a cattle prod sitting in the hall of a mansion house or a dining table complete with candles sited in a barn though both of these might be used during rituals to abuse individuals.

Rather than having a permanent set up, groups tend to be very mobile and move their venue around. They tend to keep their religious trappings carefully wrapped up and hidden at the homes of group leaders or trusted individuals. In any case, none of these artefacts would be recognised for what they really are even if someone discovered them. Neither would they ever be associated with abuse, unless someone had good reason to check them thoroughly for forensic evidence, as they are only artefacts. These artefacts would only be viewed as suspicious, if they were discovered being used during rituals.

Many survivors of this abuse are so confused that they may not even know where the rituals were actually carried out. Unless it all happens in places they are familiar with, they can only know what they have seen and been told. This may not always be the truth. An example of this might be taking a survivor to a beach and making them think that they are in Broughty Ferry when in reality they are in Tentsmuir. Children would rarely be allowed to know where the rituals happened unless they occur at home. More often than not, survivors are blindfolded or drugged when they are taken to different places and have no way of knowing what part of the country they are in.

As survivors get older, they often become more aware, or able to work out where they are taken. What survivors report is, they never know, in advance, where the venue is. The same places may be repeatedly used but never in any regular fashion.

## Tayside ➢

This section is written with the intention of making readers aware of the fact that abuse can, and does, happen in places we know. This includes Tayside in Scotland. Abuse can take place within a family home, without the awareness or involvement of parents. It can also take place in a highly organized manner in churches, halls, schools, clubs and other places where people often meet or work, without their knowledge. Naming the places used for abusing survivors does not necessarily mean or imply that the people who use, meet, live or work in any of these places are abusers themselves or in any way involved in ritual abuse. Rather, it means that abusers are clever people and often find the ways and means of getting access to a wide variety of different places. Survivors of ritual abuse have provided the following information and while I believe what survivors say to me, I have no means of proving or disproving any of it.

As I have, over the years, accumulated quite a lot of knowledge about group activities in the area in which I work, I might as well share some of that knowledge here. Not surprisingly, I have heard the same family names recurring again and again. These same names cut across different generations of people and are revealed by survivors from different backgrounds and areas. These survivors are not associated, with or known to each other. For reasons of confidentiality (and also so that I cannot be sued by anyone) I will not reveal any of the many names, I have heard, in this book. Suffice it to say that it is extremely interesting how the same abusers are repeatedly named and the same family names crop up. Abusive traditional families can easily be traced and identified by putting together pieces of information provided by several survivors.

While knowing who some of these alleged abusers are, does not in any way prove what they are doing, it is still of interest and potentially useful. It does for example, provide a way of getting closer to knowing who some of the survivors might be. By getting closer to some of the survivors, there is more of a chance that they can be helped to escape from the group. Also, knowing who some of the abusers are, increases the chances of interfering with some of their activities. This may not stop them but it will slow them down. Also, if supporters of survivors, with the permission of the survivors, begin to write down and keep details of the abusers, some day, this information may come together in a productive way.

I am certain that if the supporters of ritual abuse survivors were to pool the information they have, while obviously keeping confidentiality for the survivors, an interesting picture could be built up of group activities and membership of such groups across Scotland and more widely. Perhaps someone, someday will be interested enough in the activities of organised abusers to do this? In the meantime I will play it safe here and share a little of the information that I have. Obviously the validity of this information cannot be proven here and I make no claims to knowing everything that goes on. This is merely a small part of the knowledge I currently have. This chapter contains details, supplied by different survivors, who have given me their permission to reveal the information in this book.

I will focus here on the places that survivors say they have been taken to for group purposes in order to give the reader some idea of the extent of the areas involved. Again, survivors, even those who come from other areas including England and Wales, identify the same places, as survivors from Scotland, time and time again. Survivors have, over the years, spoken about several different groups operating in the same towns, doing the same sort of things but holding slightly different ideologies.

In Dundee for example, survivors have spoken about the presence of two satanic groups affiliated to slightly different orders, a pagan group, a quasi-Christian group and at least one Masonic group all of whom are abusive. In Perth, there is talk of at least three abusive satanic groups and a quasi-Christian group meeting regularly in the City and in the surrounding countryside I am told there are several groups. In Angus, it is difficult from the disclosures of survivors to count the actual number of groups, as they appear to cross over much more than in some other areas, and some of the same people appear to belong to more than one group. (Perhaps this is due to the rural setting?). There are however at least three independent groups existing in the small town of Arbroath and one that has been spoken about in the small town of Kirriemuir.

Though all these groups are autonomous, they do quite often cross over and come together for joint ceremonies and rituals. This can happen with groups within the same town or it can be several groups coming together for ritual purposes and abusive practices from across different areas. Occasionally, survivors talk about travelling quite far across the country to attend ritual ceremonies, which involve several groups and at which there can be over one hundred people present.

Survivors have, over many years, named some very specific places in and around Tayside and other areas. These places may have been used once or repeatedly and there is no way of saying whether or not the people who actually owned these places ever knew the purpose they were being used for. There is also no way of saying here exactly when these places were used. It would be unlikely that these places are still being used today, but feel free to keep your eyes open if you are ever in any of the areas and report to the police immediately if you happen upon any illegal activities.

Survivors have reported several specific lodges and clubs, which have been used in and around Dundee, Perth, Arbroath and Montrose. Over many years, all have been specifically named as places that survivors have been taken to, in order to be abused by groups and sometimes by individual abusers. While I cannot name these places specifically in this book suffice it to say that the Masonic connection is a fairly common theme spoken about with many survivors of ritual abuse.

Churches and church halls in Dundee's west end and on particular housing estates in the City have been spoken about in quite specific detail. Survivors have spoken about their group getting easy access to these places and sometimes using these premises for the specific purpose of desecrating and demeaning the Christian faith. Several examples given by survivors have indicated the practice in some groups of using these places around Halloween, Easter and other specific times. Survivors have spoken about being forced to be members, as children, of particular Christian churches, which they have then been taken back to by the group, or individuals for abusive and ritual purposes.

Some survivors have, in the past, named an area round Dalclaverhouse in Dundee as being extensively used by abusive groups that they were involved with. In that particular area survivors have identified, some surrounding woodlands, a large house, a church, several old cottages, an old mill and an old school

house building as places they were taken to and places where some of the actual abusers lived or worked in at the time. Some of these places are now demolished and some have been converted into flats.

The Mains Castle (as a ruin at the time), its 'across the wee burn' old and no longer used cemetery with its fallen down headstones used as altars, and the twin ponds nearby, which is quite close to the Dalclaverhouse area, was also used, according to survivors, very regularly for specific gatherings of local groups. This sort of place would have been ideal for such groups in the past due to its isolation.

Survivors have also spoken extensively about the Balumbie estate, also in the Dundee area. They have described the track up to the large mansion house/ hotel (subsequently burned down), the very high-walled garden area, which it was impossible to get out of, and the steep path down to the stream with the 'dungeon-like' small building built into the steep slope and the old ruined castle-like buildings nearby. Survivors from several generations have made mention of this large estate on the edge of the town where they claim abuse, murder and rituals would be performed in the ruins, gardens and around the large, old rowan tree which grew in front of the former mansion. This estate has fairly recently been turned into a golf course and the remains of the hotel are to be converted into flats. According to some survivors, people looking more closely at this particular estate would be sure to find some evidence as the abusers often used this area.

The old La Scala cinema in Dundee's west end and an old cinema in the Coldside area, have been identified as places used on several occasions for a specific local group to meet. According to the survivors, the group sometimes watched pornographic films in these places and then sexually abused the various children they had taken along for the purpose. Some survivors have indicated that some group members worked in these cinemas and therefore had easy access to the premises.

Several old mills in Dundee have also been spoken about by survivors who claim that in some of the mills used there were basement-like areas underneath the mills with either stagnant water or even streams running under them. Some of these places are described in great detail and include descriptions of drainage systems, brickwork, layout of the mills and contents in the premises.

# Where Angels Fear

Most of the places that the survivors talk about were clearly derelict or not in use at the time of the group meeting there, but others such as churches and cinemas, it is claimed, were in use in a normal way during the day but on occasion were used by the group or individuals in the evening or throughout the night.

In the Errol area, which is a largish village lying about halfway between Dundee and Perth, there are many places that survivors have talked about with fear and claim to have been taken to by their group. These places include one of the churches, an old hall, an old graveyard on the edge of the village, several houses with deep basements, farmhouses with barns and outbuildings, several woodland areas some of which are surrounded by high walls, a private estate and a large mansion house on the outskirts of the village.

Close by to Perth, lies Kinnoull Hill, which is a large, steep hill with woodlands and ancient ruins at the top. Not far from Kinnoull hill, in the direction of Dundee on a nearby hill, sits Kinfauns castle, another ancient ruin. According to survivors, groups use both of these places as venues for ritual purposes. Some survivors of this abuse claim that it is believed by the groups that a great deal of power is tapped into and utilized by the group during the ceremonies at these places. It is often claimed and taught by groups that these types of places are sacred and power is inherent and stronger in certain areas due to the presence of particular lay lines and a very ancient power which resides there.

In Perthshire, a large rural area, survivors have spoken about large houses in Perth City itself, mansions on the edge of town, farmhouses with outbuildings, the Bridge of Earn area, the Balmano area, the Murthly area, the Blairgowrie area and several private estates all being used by the groups at various times of year. Caravan parks in all areas have also had their fair share of mention by survivors.

In the Angus area so many places have been spoken about that they are almost impossible to list. This is probably due to the high number of survivors

# Where Angels Fear

I have personally encountered from across this area. Beaches, caves, woodlands, farms, cemeteries and caravan parks throughout the area are among the general places identified, as are large mansions, houses, private houses, warehouses and factories. Survivors, who grew up in these areas, or were taken there, have also made mention of many of the smaller towns and villages throughout Angus such as Edzell, Kirriemuir, Brechin, Arbroath, Forfar, Auchmithie, and Montrose.

Other areas outside of Tayside such as Fife, Central and Glasgow also get a too frequent mention in terms of places from many survivors of ritual abuse, with many talking about specific places such as Tentsmuir Forest and beach as well as a broad range of different towns and villages in these areas.

At the end of the day, abuse can take place anywhere at all including and especially within the family home of the survivor. Having said that, it is very interesting to note that, despite no contact at all between the many survivors I have worked with, the same addresses and places are repeatedly mentioned and described in detail by the survivors who grew up in the area or lived nearby, and also by those survivors who have been brought into the area from further afield.

Chapter 7

# Organisation

# Chapter 7
## Organisation

**Groups need a constant source of funds to continue to carry out their activities and they raise funds in a variety of ways depending on the skills and connections available within the membership of the group.** Some groups are funded by pornography. By allowing sexual activities involving children, animals and extremes of violent and abusive acts including murder to be filmed, groups can make a great deal of money. It is relatively easy for groups to use video equipment to record the abusive events that people will pay for, or even to find unscrupulous porn film crews prepared to make and distribute high quality pornographic movies. It is also easy these days with the use of modern technology to hide the identity of the individuals involved in these movies. As the markets for hard core and child pornography is fast growing and always keen for new videos and photographs, there is no shortage of funds from this particular source.

Many survivors talk about being used repeatedly in pornography, especially as children. They talk about being filmed taking part in sexual activities with other children, with adults and with various animals. Survivors describe every possible depraved act imaginable, and many acts that almost defy belief. This even includes the use of very young children and babies many of whom are killed during the filming. Pornography is very big business and some groups take full advantage of the market that exists for it. A great deal of the pornography is exported and group members would not be allowed to keep anything that is filmed locally or could in any way identify anyone. This would be considered too dangerous and a betrayal of the group.

Drugs are another useful source of funding for a group. Some groups are skilled enough to manufacture and prepare their own drugs and though few in power would be stupid enough to sell them on the streets themselves,  they can act as a source of supplying drugs to those higher up in the drugs trade. Some groups, because of connections to other countries, and within the criminal fraternity will fund the bulk buying of illegal drugs. They will not take the direct risks themselves but may on occasions force lower members of the group to act as carriers between countries. Drugs can be a very big business and a very lucrative business for a group who can produce the materials or fund an enterprise.

 Prostitution is another useful source of income, which many groups may use. Women and children from the group are used either with a member of the group finding and bringing the clients to them or by making them go out into the street to sell their services. Not only does this bring in some funds, but it also identifies some people who may be interested in being recruited into the group, as they tend to be like-minded. This is particularly the case with those people with a sexual preference for children. In addition to this, it can provide useful opportunities for the blackmail of prominent individuals who take up the sexual services offered by the children.

Given that the groups have a steady source of women and children, which they regard as their own property rather than as individuals with rights, they do not hesitate to use them to bring in funds. Children in particular are always in demand from those with a taste for children. Some groups will even sell their surplus, non-registered children to the highest bidder and this trafficking in children, which results in yet another source of income, sometimes sends the children out of the country. These children when they have grown up a bit and outlived the use of their buyer often end up being sold on to other people such as the makers of hard-core pornography.

Some groups are involved in the arms trade and buy and sell weapons to supplement their income. Some of this occurs at a local level but due to the high risk involved in this activity, much more tends to happen at an international level. Local groups might be more likely to invest in the illegal arms trade at a distance and through their contacts with other groups. Again, as with their other means of income generation, the groups are tapped into a wide variety of secretive networks that few ordinary people even know about.

Effectively, a highly organised criminal sub-culture exists within our society ranging from the criminals who are hired to carry out low-level activities for groups and who may not even know they are being employed by the group, to involvement in crime at a national and international level. Not all members of the group will even know about the extent of this and the knowledge will be strictly limited to a need to know basis.

Groups are connected to each other across this country and other countries, with many being affiliated to larger secret societies. Though each local group is autonomous, they do still have to operate within the fairly wide boundaries of the rules of affiliation. Most do so as there are so many benefits to be gained from being part of a larger secret organisation, not least of which is being able to tap into high-level pornography, the slave trade, the drugs and the arms markets.

Several of these larger organisations exist in this country and indeed throughout the world. Some of them openly admit to following a different faith, but totally deny involvement in abuse and criminal activity. These larger organisations are also linked to each other and though few would openly admit or acknowledge it, above them are the even more secret organisations, which only the considered elite are ever recruited into. Becoming a member of these groups is by invitation only and is only allowed after rigorous testing and proving worthy enough. Some higher-level groups consider themselves to be the people who will rule the world one day and consider this to be the right way of things.

## Organisation of Groups ➢

Abusive groups are organised in many different ways and they often use different and individual names to designate the position of those who are involved in the group. Some for example, follow the Christian method of naming individuals and positions using such terminology as high priest, priest, bishop, deacon, elder and congregation to differentiate amongst individuals and denote the hierarchy. Others use words like adept, prime, master, grand master, magister and knight. Much of the naming depends on the particular affiliation of the individual group and which particular brand of religion or beliefs they follow. Each group usually has a secret group name that only those high up in it and other associated groups will know. Most groups claim to be affiliated to wider networks and like-minded organisations, which also follow the left-hand path, as it is sometimes called.

The left hand path is generally regarded as the path of individuality, freethinking and self-discovery. Rather than being dictated to by the doctrines of others, followers of the left hand path tend towards looking within themselves for their own power and authority. They do not follow in the paths of others and instead choose and follow their own direction in life. Rather than following the will or dictates of others they follow their own will. Not all followers of the left hand path are abusive in their actions any more than followers of the right-hand path i.e. Christians, are non-abusive. People who are abusive exist on both sides of the path and those people who seek to abuse others can choose to distort any doctrine or belief system they choose to suit their own ends.

Though groups who practice ritualised abuse may often have a proper and secret name for their group or meetings, members amongst themselves often call it the Lodge, Church, Kirk, Clubbie, Chapel, or other commonly used name. This effectively helps them fit into the existing culture and also has the advantage of allowing for minor slip-ups of the children. A child saying they were at the church on Sunday is unlikely to shock anyone enough into asking any more about it. This would be perceived as a relatively normal thing for a child to say and it would normally be accepted at face value.

Each member of the group is often given a specific and secret group name, and/or identity by the group when they are first initiated into the group. This name only gets used within the group under certain ritual settings. Survivors are usually very reluctant to let other people know the name they were given by the group, because as part of the belief system it is believed that if anyone knows your secret name, they can gain power over you.

Sometimes survivors are called by a particular name during a ritual or are named during a ritual for a particular purpose, e.g. a survivor might be referred to as 'the sacrifice', 'the vessel' or 'the offering'. Some children, especially those who have not been registered at birth, are often not given a proper name at all and they (officially within the group) have a name chosen for them by the group. This name will never be a normal sounding name but may be a name of a deity of some sort e.g. Moloch or even the name of a type of animal. These children are considered to be unworthy of naming properly. Many of these children do not last long in the group in that they are used, abused and then disposed of by the group.

Many traditional groups have both a High Priest and High Priestess at the top position. Though the name used for the person or people at the top may change, e.g. they may be called master, bishop, president, eminence, or other such name, the general idea is that there is a group leader. Patriarchal groups tend to have the males in all the top positions with the occasional woman as a priestess and all other women kept in the lower orders. Matriarchal groups tend to consist of all women in the top positions of power and the groups are often all female in composition. Some groups will call themselves covens and will, for example, consist of thirteen women only, with men and children occasionally allowed to be part of the lower orders during some rituals. There can also be mixed groups in which men and women can equally compete for power and position within them.

Some groups have a small group of people just below the leaders who are also in a position of power and responsibility. Depending on the set up of the group there might be adepts who have reached the standards of learning and achievement set by the faith or there might be an group organiser, a bit like a Master of Ceremonies. This person is sometimes called the Thane in some groups. Regardless of the name or designation, most groups will have someone in this position to organise events and keep everything running smoothly. There might also be a Scribe. Most groups will have someone high up who will keep the records in order and keep the accounts of the group up to date. Often this is just one person although larger groups might have two people doing this job.

Most groups also have a person in charge of the magic. This person may be called a witch, wizard, oracle, magi or other similar name. Depending on the group, there might also be a person called the shaman who oversees rituals and makes predictions for the group. Whatever name is actually given to these people, they are generally much feared and viewed as powerful people in the group and are responsible for much of the cursing, visions, predictions, healing and ceremonial performances during rituals. In reality, these people are usually the people who have learned the ways of tricks, illusions and deceptions.

There is often, in some groups, a third order of power. Within this, depending on the group and their beliefs may be what is sometimes called the initiates or adepts. These are people who can and will aspire to a higher position in the group. They will have passed many of the tests and initiations of the group and although lower than the others are frequently ambitious in nature and design. They will have a good grounding in the faith but in order to progress in some groups, they will have to oust someone out of a higher position, this is expected of them if they are to progress. Some groups have the lower initiates below this level and these are the people who have been accepted into the group but have not yet achieved enough to be allowed into the higher or inner circles of the group.

Some groups structure themselves into an inner and outer circle and each circle also has its own hierarchy within it. The inner circle consists of those in the top positions and the outer circle consists of those in lower position and who are considered not yet worthy enough or learned enough to be allowed to know certain group secrets. Even within these groups, there are those people who belong to the group but are not ever allowed to enter even the outer circle of the group.

In some groups, they even run to a congregation consisting of what is seen as the lower orders of people. Some of these will be the partners of group members with position, some may be some of the older children who are destined for a position, and some may be women kept for the purpose of providing children for the group. Sometimes, groups allow like-minded people to become part of the congregation with the view to more actively recruiting them into the group through time. None of these people will ever be allowed to know much of the real workings of the group until they have passed through various stages of initiation and can be trusted more fully. Given that all of these people will be involved in serious crimes long before they ever get near to an initiation, it is unlikely that they will ever reveal anything about the group. To do so would be to incriminate himself or herself, as much as anyone else. In addition to this, these are people who usually enjoy abusing others and it suits them to be a part of this type of situation.

Regardless of how the group is structured at the bottom there are always people who exist only to serve the purpose of the group. In many groups, they are not even regarded as people at all and are treated like slaves. These are mainly children, some of them unregistered, young adults with no position or power and a few adults often kept only while they are in some way useful to the group. Very few from this group of people ever reach adulthood, none will ever gain in position or power and all are regarded as the belongings of the group. Even human slavery in all its worst possible forms can never compare to the kind of lives that these people lead. They exist only to suffer, be used by all group members and eventually die for the group.

## The Fringes ➢

There are many people who are not directly members of abusive groups but who are closely linked to the groups and sit on the fringes of many of the group activities. Some of these people work for the groups, receive an income from the groups for services rendered, buy such things as pornography, or even children from the groups and are involved to a greater or lesser degree with groups. Occasionally some of these individuals are allowed, at a price, to join in some of the group activities particularly those activities, which involve sexually abusing children. Seldom are they allowed into the religious activities of the group unless they are becoming involved more fully, or are seeking to join the group as a full member.

Some individuals are employed by the group as security guards and they are well paid to keep watch for anyone taking too much of an interest in the group activities. Though they may not be aware of everything that is occurring during rituals, they are most certainly aware of the fact that criminal activities are taking place. They themselves are usually criminals and allowing them to abuse some of the individuals in the group implicates them in the acts of abuse. This, in addition to paying them for the security they provide, ensures their continued loyalty and complete silence.

Some, who are not group members may also be involved in such things as pornography and prostitution. Camera crews consisting of like-minded individuals are brought in to make the pornographic films involving the abuse of children. Children are sometimes sold to individuals to be used sexually and taken back into the group when the children become older and past their usefulness to that individual. There are also the many individuals who buy the child pornography produced by the groups, who though not directly involved in abusing the children, continue to create a demand for the abusive materials.

All these individuals, though not part of the actual group, do have a vested interest in maintaining the silence and keeping abusive groups going. Many of these individuals are respected members of the community and as they come from all walks of life, they represent a very broad section of society.

The groups from time to time, in any number of ways in order to advance the purposes and will of the group use these people on the fringes. Groups keep detailed records of all the people involved on the fringe so that, if they ever need something from them, they have willing allies. If the person is less than willing to be an ally, the group, to make them comply with any requests for assistance, can very easily blackmail them with the information they hold about them. Fringe people can, for example, if they work in an area that group members would benefit from, be called upon to carry out a small task that could only be done by someone in their position. If they work even as a clerk in the Benefits, Housing or Health services, files can easily be accessed and information be gained about an individual, or go missing, to cause disruption to an individual.

Some of these fringe people will, through time, join the group properly. Many others will just not have the courage to get fully involved though they will continue to enjoy the fringe benefits. Some of them will simply not be considered by the group to be good enough to become full members and will be kept firmly out. Though many of these people will have little in common, other than a lack of basic human decency, one thing that all fringe members do have in common is that they will know very little that can incriminate the group. No group would ever trust the people on the fringes with any real or relevant information, which they might be able to use against the group. All of them are kept firmly in the dark unless there is something that they need to know in order to carry out a task for the group.

Without these criminals on the fringes of the groups, many activities of the group would just not happen, nor ever be sustained. It is the fringe element that creates the steady demand for many of the products of the groups and finances the groups to a high degree. While these people may not be directly responsible for some of the abuse of survivors, their constant demands for such things as pornography, snuff movies and access to children, encourages groups to sink to ever increasing degrees of depravity and causes greater abuse and torture of the survivors. Without these people on the fringes, groups would still continue to do what they do in the name of their religion and because they like to have power over other people, but the extent of what they do would be far less than it is now.

# Chapter 8
# Common Objects associated with Rituals

Chapter 8
**Common Objects
associated with
Rituals**

**ROBES:** Most survivors of ritual abuse talk of the abusers wearing robes of different kinds during the ceremonies. This is, in many ways, similar to some Christian church ceremonies during which the officials dress up to add dignity and seriousness to the proceedings. Survivors' talk about ceremonial robes of different colours, with different coloured trimmings round them being worn by those in different positions and with different skills in groups. During specific ceremonies, at different times of the year, the group members may wear slightly different robes, depending on the event they are celebrating. This changing of robes for a different ritual is particularly the case with those in high positions of authority and power in the group.

Often there is a hierarchy in the colours but as this differs so much between groups there is no hard and fast way of determining the hierarchy of a group and colours used by them other than by asking individual survivors about how it worked in their own group. Having said that, red and black are most often spoken about in terms of a holder of high position and purple, gold and silver often denote power and authority in many groups. Many survivors do not like these colours at all, particularly in combination with each other and some survivors show intense fear of some colours, particularly the colours red and black together.

# Where Angels Fear

Occasionally the robes spoken about have large open hoods, which the wearers may pull over their heads. This makes it difficult to see the faces of the wearer and sometimes survivors, especially child survivors will describe the abusers as being faceless because they did not see a face. The robes, especially when worn with the hoods covering the head and face make it almost impossible for the survivor to recognise the individual abusers until they are removed. Sometimes those higher up in the group also wear chains of office and other such regalia to add to the pomp of the occasion. The robes are worn to frighten, disguise and add ceremony and credibility to the proceedings. No clothing is generally worn under the robes and they are often completely abandoned as the ritual progresses.

Survivors are also often dressed in robes at first. These are also of a particular colour to denote position or denote what the survivor is to be used for. An example of this could be to dress a survivor in white to indicate the survivor as a sacrifice or dress them in **grey to indicate betrayal** of the group at other times, the survivor will wear whatever colour their own rank decrees e.g. green as indicating having some power and position or blue indicating the lower orders of the group.

**MASKS:** Many groups make use of masks of different sorts to hide their identity, add to the fear or depict various demons or animals. These masks are often very life-like and sometimes there is a costume worn to go with the mask. Sometimes there are devices or padding inside the mask which changes and muffles the voice of the person wearing it. For children, this is especially frightening and confusing, as younger children often believe that it really is the demon or an animal that is abusing them. Then if they try to tell about it, which is wholly unlikely, they will talk about being hurt by a tiger or a devil with horns for example. This makes their story sound extraordinary and too incredible to be believed.

**ALTAR:** Most groups use an altar as central to the rituals they carry out. The altar is most often made of stone and may be covered by a specially designed cloth, painted or inscribed for the ceremonial occasion. Runes and symbols are generally drawn or written on the altar or on the cloth draped over it. The altar is usually adult sized and big enough for a person to lie down on. On occasions, smaller child-sized altars are used for particular rituals. The altar is used in a variety of ways including for ceremonial rape of individuals, sacrifice of animals, blood letting of people and even for murder. Sometimes individuals are strapped or chained to the altar while rites are performed to them and around them and although many other abuses may be going on around the periphery, the event held at the altar is often regarded as the main event and the climax of the occasion.

**CANDLES:** To add atmosphere to the rituals being performed, candles are frequently burned around the arena. They may be black, red, made of animal or human fat or mixed with blood. Frequently herbs are added to the candles to create a heady smell and produce intoxication in the room. Symbols and runes are often carved into the candles to symbolise the events taking place. Sometimes marked candles are used to mark the time when specific things will happen during the ritual. These candles burn down to the allocated mark and this keeps the members to the right time for the rituals to be performed. Through use of chemicals, the candles can be made to burn with an unusual colour and flame, which the abusers will claim to be the result of their great magic and power.

**BOWLS AND CHALICES:** These are often similar to some Christian artefacts and are often made of silver, and sometimes of gold. They are generally inscribed with runes and symbols and are very ornate in appearance. These are usually only handled by those who are high in power in the group. They are commonly used to collect the blood, which is let during the rituals. As part of the ritual, this blood may be used to draw symbols on people and objects, and there is usually a communal and symbolic drinking of the blood. Other body fluids may also be collected in these and used in rituals.

**DAGGERS, SWORDS AND KNIVES:** Ceremonial daggers, swords and knives used by those in high office are a common feature during rituals. Like the other artefacts they are generally highly ornate and may be decorated with such things as snakes, skulls, crosses, stars and demonic looking creatures. They are used to draw blood, to mutilate and kill animal sacrifices and sometimes even people. Some groups use specific weapons for different things i.e. a specific dagger to draw blood as an offering to a deity and a different knife to kill. Groups vary in this practice but survivors may fear the sight of one specific kind of weapon over another as they associate it with a particular act of abuse.

**HORNS:** These may be the carved horns of a sheep, a goat or another horned creature and are sometimes well decorated with silver trimmings. Sometimes groups may use them simply to add to the atmosphere of the occasion but commonly they may be used to hurt, frighten and abuse others. Some groups have them sharpened at the edge or tip so as to easily cut and draw blood with them and/or they may also be used for sexual purposes and inserted into body orifices. During the height of ceremonies and rituals, some sexually aroused individuals may use them willingly on themselves. Sometimes, they are strapped onto abusers and used to simulate intercourse with a deity. Sometimes female abusers use them to penetrate others. The survivors are usually the unwilling participants in these acts.

**BELLS:** Some survivors talk about the use of silver or gold bells in calling them to attention, as a warning or in training them in how to behave for the occasion. Some talk of the use of a single or double ring to denote what is about to occur or how they must respond at any one time.

A simple example of this could be that on one ring of the bell they must lie down, two rings means they must stand up. In reality, survivors frequently talk about much more serious things than lying down or standing up. The main thing about it is that they are often taught to react instantly in a pre-programmed way to a stimulus such as the ring of a bell. Any failure to react immediately in the way the abusers have dictated and taught brings instant and severe punishment.

**BONES AND SKULLS:** During rituals there may be human and animal bones on display and used for specific purposes. This can range from the use of finger bones for the casting of runes and spells to skulls used as chalices. Some of these bones may be quite old and ornately carved. They may have belonged to the group for a very long time and been passed down through generations of worshippers. There may be the claim that they contain a very powerful magic or they may be used in a traditional way within a group. Other bones may be prepared specifically for an occasion or even during an occasion. Again they are intended to add to the fear and mystique and portray the group as extremely powerful and capable of doing anything. To make use of human bones, especially the bones of an infant, is to go against all moral teachings, behaviours and beliefs in the nature of humanity and reverence for those who have died. Effectively, this is exactly what the group intends.

**INSECTS AND CREEPY CRAWLIES:** Such as maggots, wasps, bees, slugs, ants, worms and spiders are all used by groups to frighten, punish, break down resistance and degrade individuals. The individual may be confined with the creatures, may be forced to consume them, have them placed inside body orifices or a multitude of other uses may be made of them. To show their power over insects, a group member may perform a ritual, which appears to cause the insects to swarm in a particular direction and even onto an identified individual. That this is a trick usually involving smearing the person with chemicals, which the insects are attracted to, is usually lost to the person (especially if they are children) being terrorised by the insects and the abusers. They are usually left with the belief that the abusers' even have power over insects and their fear of the abusers intensifies accordingly.

**ANIMALS:** Are used in a variety of ways by abusive groups. They may be used as a live sacrifice during a ritual to be tortured, mutilated and killed or used to enhance the group power. Dogs may be trained to guard the children and stop them if they try to run away. They, and other animals may be trained with the help of chemical stimulants to act out sexually with people including children. Some group members will willingly perform sexual acts with animals but other times, the animals are used to sexually abuse individuals. This may occur as part of a ritual or it may be used for pornographic purposes. These individuals are often restrained by group members or tied so they cannot move and the animal excited by the chemicals smeared on the person is encouraged to perform a sexual act upon the individual.

**CURSE DOLLS AND OBJECTS:** Many groups make use of a belief in their ability to curse and cause harm to others even at a distance. Sometimes this is performed through the use of curse dolls. An object belonging to the person or a part of the person's DNA such as hair, nail clippings or similar substances are used in order to carry out the curse. Elaborate rituals are performed using the object and a person is cursed. Within the group, such is the belief in this power to curse others and cause them harm that frequently survivors believe that the group can reach them anywhere. A survivor suffering from a flashback may believe that the group has laid a curse upon them and caused the flashback to happen to them. As flashbacks can feel exactly like reliving an actual abusive act, this belief can cause the survivor to think that they are still being abused and attacked by the group. Anything bad that happens to a survivor will often be put down to such a curse being laid upon them by the group.

**CROSS:** Many groups make use of a cross but they invert it. Often they hang their human sacrifices upside down on the inverted cross and abuse or even kill them. Killing is often done by cutting the throat of the victim and draining their blood. Prior to the killing, the hair is often cut or the head shaved so as not to interfere with the blood flow. The other common practice is to give the person something such as Warferin, beforehand to stop the blood from clotting at all and then making a cut that allows the person to slowly bleed to death. Sometimes, people are hung

upside down on the crosses for long periods of time while other rituals are taking place or as a prelude to abusing them further in different ways. The inverted cross is a symbol of the turning round of Christianity and the complete dismissal of it as a power to be reckoned with.

Smaller hand held crosses are also used in rituals to sexually penetrate survivors, including children, and children are frequently forced or encouraged to use these and other similar objects on each other in a sexual way.

**GROUP BIBLE:** No ritual ceremony would ever be complete without the accompanying holy book. This is often a large book bound (so it is claimed) in human skin and read from by the high priest or other presiding officer. The book is usually written in an ancient language such as Latin and in a similar way to other religions there is often a call by the priest and a response expected back from the congregation during the worship. There are usually other books to accompany the main book and group members will have smaller religious books of their own which they must study and live their lives according to.

**FIRE:** This is often a component of ritual abuse and ranges from the use of hand held fire torches to using larger fires and bonfires. In many groups, they celebrate one or more of the fire festivals throughout the year and during these, large bonfires are a major feature of the ceremony. Some groups use the fire to ritualistically burn their enemies, some use it as part of initiation into the group, others use it to frighten and control children and adults. They may threaten to burn the person and on occasions actually do so. Adult survivors sometimes talk of witnessing children and adults being put into the fire and burned to death.

Other kinds of fire are also used to prove the power of the group. Members of the group appear to be able to walk unscathed through fire, fire is made to change its colour and properties e.g. rather than hot, it burns cold, and the high priest can often make the fire go out or in again with a word or gesture. To the children and those who have no means of questioning how all of this works, this display of apparently awesome magic is extremely powerful.

No one can ever blame a survivor for believing that the group has the ability and power to control fire as they have seen with their own eyes and experienced for themselves the many strange things that have occurred with fire. Yet, all of this so-called magic is based on deception and tricks with only a chosen few privy to the secrets of how it works. As with modern day illusionists and magicians, the finer workings of such clever deceptions is a closely guarded secret that is kept at the highest level of the group.

**TARPAULIN:** It is common these days, for groups to make use of places where they have to rapidly put everything back in order and leave not a shred of evidence behind them. As a result of this, many groups have a large sheet of tarpaulin that they take with them when they go to a group ceremony. Acts that lead to the spilling of blood, semen and excrement are always performed within the boundaries of the tarpaulin, which is then, when the group is finished, simply rolled up and removed from the scene afterwards. This can then be taken, with its evidence intact, to a safe place for proper cleaning.

**SYMBOLS:** Groups make liberal use of different symbols to depict such things as, what the ceremony is about, what is to occur during it and who and what is to be involved in it.

Children learn very quickly what the symbols mean, even if they are not formally taught them. If each time they see a particular symbol they witness a child raped, tortured or killed, they quickly begin to realise that the particular symbol drawn on the wall means a child will be raped, tortured or die over the course of the next few days. As everything is carefully orchestrated ahead of time, the key players i.e. those at the top know what is to unfold and depict it around the area. Adult members will all know and be able to read the symbols, as will some of the children who have been taught the meaning.

Children, who are not taught, soon learn from the symbols they see and can work out what the outcomes will be. The difference with the children is that they rarely know in advance exactly who is going to be on the receiving end of the particular abuse that they see symbolised. This leaves the children with such a heightened fear of extreme torture and death that they quickly become relieved, and almost welcoming of the rapes, beatings and depravity they do suffer. At least this time round they did not die. Relief can quickly turn to intense gratitude and they then become more willing to serve the abusers rather than suffer the same fate as the others before them. Sometimes children are told they are to be the sacrifice, and are taken right through the sacrificial ceremony until they become totally accepting of their fate. Right at the end, the abusers sometimes turn this around, and suddenly release the child and choose another child to take its place. The released child is left relieved, disappointed and shocked at the outcome.

The reason the child is relieved is obvious. Less obvious are the feelings of disappointment and shock. These feelings come mainly from the child having reached a stage of resignation and acceptance in the inevitability of death. Also, because the child is hurting so much, is exhausted and cannot take any more, the child begins to feel that death would be welcome. To the child, death at this point in time would mean an end to the suffering.

In addition to all of this, comes the guilt. Survivors often begin to feel extremely guilty that they survived at all. This is a common theme with adult survivors who talk about how worthless they are and their willingness to die rather than go on enduring the pain. They can often feel guilty that they felt relieved when another child was chosen or took their place. Many also find it difficult to come to terms with the fact that they survived when others did not.

Because symbols hold such huge meaning for survivors, they are often used after survivors escape to frighten and terrorise them into returning to the group. These symbols may be drawn and passed on to the survivor and the fear caused by receiving such a symbol is so great that survivors cannot help reacting to the sight of them. The symbols tell the survivor what is expected of them and what will happen if they do not comply with the instructions of the group. Experience will have taught them that non-compliance with group instructions is extremely dangerous. Experience will also have taught them that to be given a particular symbol is effectively to receive a sentence of death. This causes real terror in the survivor. It is little wonder that they begin to associate particular symbols with particular events and think that they have no choice but to obey.

Many survivors of ritual abuse are conditioned to react to a variety of symbols in different ways. Symbols are used extensively during the ceremonies carried out by groups to add to the mystique and supposed gravity of the event and as survivors learn, while still quite young, to understand the meaning of the different symbols, many can become very afraid, even many years after leaving the abuse, if they as much as see the symbols drawn anywhere.

# Chapter 9
# Children involved in Ritual Abuse

Chapter 9
## Children involved in Ritual Abuse

**As we all know, children are extremely vulnerable and totally dependent on the adults in their lives to care for them and protect them from harm**. The younger the child, the more dependent and more vulnerable they are. Most people never think about the abuse of children unless it directly affects them and even fewer people ever hear about, or think about, ritualised abuse. Many of those who do hear about it dismiss it as fantasy, fabrication or something that could never happen in their own area or to their own child.

Most parents do care for their children and do succeed in protecting them from harm but sometimes abusers are clever enough to get through the defences of even the most protective of parents and manage to abuse children. Such is the skill of the abusers in completely silencing the children and covering their tracks, that this abuse is rarely disclosed at the time and parents often remain completely unaware of it for many years afterwards. Abuse is rarely discovered without the survivor actually disclosing that it is happening or has happened to them. Children involved in ritual abuse rarely disclose it to anyone and even when they do, the things that the children speak about, often sound so unbelievable that people often disregard or do not understand what the child is saying and the abuse remains largely undetected.

Unfortunately, some children are born to parents who have little or no interest in their welfare and no desire at all to protect them from harm. Sometimes, some parents are simply inadequate, neglectful or ignorant of the need to protect their child from harm. Some parents go further than this and quite simply do not care at all about the welfare of their child. They have no parental feelings to speak of and do nothing at all to safeguard the child. Children in this situation are completely unprotected by the adults they are totally dependent on and this makes for even greater vulnerability.

Some parents even go so far as to choose to have children in order to use and abuse them. They deliberately form relationships for the purpose and deliberately have children with the intention of using and abusing them. If someone has the tendency and desire to abuse children, the easiest way to get easy access to them in private is to produce them for themselves. That people are capable of doing this is sometimes difficult for good and moral people to understand as they find it incomprehensible to think and believe that anyone could choose to have children in order to hurt and abuse them. Unfortunately, some abusers actually do this.

There are many different ways that young children can become involved in the activities of a group practising ritual abuse. Abusers, particularly those who are involved with groups of like-minded individuals who practise ritual abuse, are always very keen to get their hands on young children. Frequently, the members of a group deliberately produce children for the group to use. They use the women within their groups, either willingly or unwillingly, as vessels, which they can impregnate and thus, in time, provide live babies. The woman may be kept hidden from public sight as her pregnancy develops so that no one outside of the group will know that she is even pregnant. Providing she is not a person who would be missed by anyone, it is relatively easy to keep her out of circulation for a few months. On other occasions, a woman may carry the child openly and later tell people that she has miscarried the child or that the child was stillborn. Certainly no one would ever think to check out her story.

If a woman never attends a doctor or a hospital during her pregnancy, she can quite easily carry a child to full term and produce a child who, to all intents and purposes, does not publicly exist. Abusive groups often have access to a doctor who is fully committed to the purposes of the group and will tend pregnant women and officiate, if need be, at the birth. There would be no official records of such a child anywhere, no records of pregnancy, no registration of a birth, no birth certificate, no medical card, nothing. The only people who would know that the child had ever been born at all would be the woman herself and those involved in the group. Given that the intention of these people is to cause harm to the child, they are hardly likely to tell anyone outside the group that the child even existed. This leaves the child totally at the mercy of the members of the group.

The woman herself may be fully involved in the group and, having chosen to give the child to the group, could never tell. This would be tantamount to a confession of guilt that she has willingly broken the law and abused her child. Sometimes the woman is too afraid to try and tell about the birth, as she believes herself to be to blame and culpable and fears the consequences of a disclosure too much. The abusers will have been certain to ensure that the woman feels responsible and guilty, even although, for some, they have absolutely no choice in what has happened. This guilt adds to her silence though and safeguards the abusers from disclosure and discovery.

Other women may be so totally controlled by the abusive group that they are effectively rendered permanently silent. They may be in the position of being so controlled that they are allowed little or no access to the outside world. They may be so traumatised that they cannot talk about what happened for many years, if ever. They may suffer from learning difficulties or be so damaged by the abuse that they are not capable of ever telling. They may even simply believe that there is no one they can ever tell, have no trust in anyone and/or believe that it is useless to try and tell about the child. At the end of the day, even if any of the women were able to tell about the child, few would ever be believed and the evidence in the shape of a child would be long gone. Many adult survivors who have succeeded in escaping from groups and begun to try and talk about the children they have had, or known about, can testify to this.

Many children produced in this way are subjected to extremes of torture, mutilation and eventual murder with no one ever able or willing to admit that they ever existed in the first place. Few of these children ever live longer than the first few years of life and it is very rare for one of them to reach adulthood.

Those who do are often so badly damaged mentally and physically that they cannot live independently of the group. They certainly would not normally have the capacity to escape from the group or be able to tell anyone about their suffering.

Many babies are deliberately induced early so they can be used at particular ritual events. Some of these babies are induced too early to be viable and would never be able to live. They are certainly not given the chance to live long by the group. Others, if provided with swift medical help, would be able to survive despite being induced early. They are not provided with this help as they have been produced for the sole purpose of death. Some are taken to full-term and allowed to live for a little while until the group needs them for a ritual or for pornography. No matter what stage the pregnancy is allowed to go to before birth, the vast majority of these children are doomed from the minute they are conceived.

## Born into it ➢

Some children are born into the culture and tradition of ritual abuse. One or both parents may be active members of a group and be quite accepting of involving their children in the activities of the group. Not only do they allow their child to be actively used in terrifying rituals and ceremonies involving extremes of physical and sexual abuse, but usually, they also reinforce the message of silence and compliance within the home setting on a daily basis. Parents such as this, no matter what belief system they employ to justify their behaviour, benefit financially and personally from the abuse that their child suffers. Like most abusers, particularly those who belong to organised groups, these parents will rarely be brought to justice. Currently, the best that can be hoped for is that the child, for some reason will be removed from them before too much damage is done.

Children born into and raised in such families are taught from a very early age that the lives they are leading are right and proper. Long before they reach school age they have been taught the rules of silence and the many traditions of the group. In the same way that any child growing up within a religious family is taught and conditioned to accept the faith of the parents,

**DUNDEE YOUNG WOMEN'S CENTRE**

so too are these children. They will be taught the group version of history, the philosophy of their religion, languages, what is expected of them and the implications of ever telling about the group or the religion. They have absolutely no choice in any of this. Neither can they ever know or begin to understand, while young, that what they are experiencing is completely unacceptable within society. To these children their lives are normal to them and they have nothing else to begin to compare it with.

It is only when children get older, if they are given/allowed enough freedom, that they are able to begin to question whether or not there is any other way to live. By then, they are so thoroughly silenced and conditioned, that it is unlikely they will ever try to tell anyone or seek help from anyone. While young, children have absolutely no choice in how they live and no matter whether they question what is going on, or not, they are well and truly stuck in the situation.

Depending on the family these children are born into, the child may feel that they have too much to lose by telling. Some, even while still quite young, will have given in and accepted their roles and position within the group. Few consider what is happening to themselves and others to be abuse but rather they accept things as right because their parents and their faith dictates it as such. For some, they have too much to gain from the group to ever risk exposure. If they themselves are destined to win a position of power within the group, they very quickly reap the rewards of behaving as they have been taught to behave. Some of these children grow up to be the next generation of abusers.

Some of those children born into the faith are regarded purely as property to be used by the parents and the group in whatever way they want. They are not destined to gain in power or position and are taught from an early age that they are completely worthless and should be grateful for ever being allowed to live. These children are very much controlled by the family and the group to the extent that they may be kept totally dependent on the group for all things.

## Single parent marries into it ➤

There are, these days, an increasing number of single parent families as it is now more acceptable to leave partners and bring up children alone. Abusers often actively seek out and pursue a relationship with single parents in order to get access to their children. So too with abusers who are involved with ritual abuse. Single parents, who are usually women, sometimes become involved with men who are, unknown to them at the time,

involved with an abusive group. These women, over time, may become victims of the brainwashing and abuse that frequently characterises domestic violence and become less able to protect their children. They may be totally taken in by the man and not know that he has set out to abuse the children.

The children in such a situation quickly become isolated from their mother and are carefully 'groomed' and prepared to become involved in the group activities. Usually, the abuser takes everything very slowly and gently at first so as to gradually introduce and accustom the child to its new situation. Over time, as the child becomes accustomed to accepting more and more in the way of abuse and ritual, the child is exposed to more until they accept anything that is done to them and other children. As the silencing of the children is always an absolute priority so as to ensure the safety of the abusers, long before any extremes of abuse take place; the children will know not to talk to anyone about what is going on.

## Close relative or family friend takes them in ➤

Some children are introduced to ritual abuse through close relatives or family friends. As the parents trust these people, they can often have easy access to the children from quite an early age. Like many child abusers, they ingratiate themselves into families with young children and are quickly regarded as being 'good with children'. They offer to look after the children, take them on holiday and generally succeed in spending a great deal of time alone with the children. This provides them with adequate time and opportunity to begin to abuse the children. Again, silencing the child is the key to allowing

DUNDEE YOUNG WOMEN'S CENTRE

this to continue and they generally progress slowly towards more frequent and more extremes of abuse.

As the parent trusts the abuser, the child can easily be persuaded that the parent has permitted all of what is going on. Young children are seldom able to work out for themselves the validity of this. All they will know is that they are repeatedly handed over to the abuser and their parent seems quite happy with this. They will also see that the parent is friendly with and accepting of the abuser. Few young children would ever seek to question this. A child in this situation does at least have a sense of normality at home but this can serve to make everything more confusing as the child slips from one reality to another.

## Foster carers ➤

For a variety of reasons children are sometimes placed in foster care for a period of time. Some can be in foster care for quite a long period of time from infancy until they move on to other carers, back to their parents or are placed for adoption. Some abusers gain access to these children by becoming foster carers. Although all foster carers have to pass stringent safety checks by social services before being allowed to care for children, some abusers can easily pass these checks as they have never been caught, reported or prosecuted for any abuse of children. Many abusers appear on the surface to be upright and respectable people until such time as a child or adult survivor finds the strength and courage to speak out against them.

Those foster carers who are part of groups who practise ritual abuse usually involve their foster children in the abuse also. It is a case of 'too good an opportunity' to miss. Though the abuse experienced by these children is extremely traumatic, because there is involvement with outside agencies and the possibility of the child moving on to a new home at some point, the abusers are careful to abuse the children in more subtle ways. Abusers are careful to make certain that the children can be thoroughly silenced before and after abuse and a huge emphasis is placed on ensuring continuing silence. These children are often repeatedly drugged and hypnotised, subjected to extreme sensory deprivation and tricked and confused by constant deceptions. The end result is often a silent, overly fearful child who is unable to make any sense of what they have experienced.

It is often a long time before these children can begin to remember or talk coherently about their experiences. Often their memories are very shattered and confused and the pieces they do remember are unable to fit into any order or make much sense to them or anyone else. Because of the confusion and lack of clear and coherent memories, the children can rarely give adequate details of what actually happened to them. Also, because the abusers will have deliberately deceived them, much of what the child is able to say sounds so bizarre that it is unlikely to be believed or be clear enough for any non-abusive adult to begin to understand what actually happened. The only thing that may be really clear is that the child is so traumatised that something terrible must have happened to them.

Often children who have gone into foster care are distressed to start with and sometimes the assumption is made that a distressed or disturbed child in care is nothing to do with the lack of care they receive but more to do with their troubled backgrounds. Seldom are there any thoughts by anyone of suspecting the foster carers of abuse. Yet many adult survivors of a range of different abuses talk about being abused while in foster care. Abusers can be in any position and what better position could an abuser get into than being the foster carer of a vulnerable child.

## Child minders ➤

Many children go regularly, and increasingly these days, sometimes for long periods of time to child-minders as their parents work full-time. The vast majority of these child-minders are very good and caring of the children and would never permit harm to come to the children in their care. As with foster carers, registered child-minders in this country are carefully checked out and vetted by the authorities and this is, to a point, a good safeguard for children. However, abusers come from all walks of life and few are ever caught and convicted of offences against children. Just because someone has been checked out by local authorities does not necessarily mean that they may not involve a child in abuse.

Some adult survivors talk about having been involved in ritual abuse through their regular child-minder. These people may not be as likely to be able to take the children into all of the activities of the group, and they have to be very careful to make sure that the child will not talk, is not bruised and that there is no visible evidence that might make a parent suspicious. On occasions, some children do tell their parents what has happened to them, but the things they say can be so bizarre that they are often put down to children's fantasy and imagination.

Though children abused in this way are usually out of it by the time they get to school age and often have the advantage of having good parents and a good home to return to, the trauma to them is not lessened. In many ways, it can be very difficult for the survivors as they get older and remember what went on, to believe themselves that such strange things could have happened to them. They often doubt their own memory of the events even as adults. They remember what happened in a small child-like fashion sometimes with no language to know what was actually being done to them or why it was happening to them. They also have no context to place it in or any understanding of what the abusers were doing and why. All they have is a jumble of memories in which adults acted differently from others and sometimes hurt or frightened them.

## Experiences of child survivors ➢

Obviously a great deal depends on the age of a child, their understanding and their development stage but with ritual abuse, the experience of a child can also be about what level of involvement they will have had both with individual abusers and the abusive group. Often, this is dictated by whether or not their parents or carers are themselves involved and what position, if any, they are destined to hold in a group. Children who are involved at a superficial level i.e. being brought in occasionally by adults, who have managed to gain some access to them, are used and abused in a more general way than those who are being trained to play a fuller role in the group life and ritual. They know less about the group and what it is all about and the frightening rituals and the abuse they experience and witness are the key elements and trauma for them.

All children involved in any way with ritual abuse are subject to threats both to themselves and others, displays of total power and control and emotional and physical violence. All will be made to witness extreme acts and all will be taught under pain of torture and death not to talk or tell anyone about their experiences. The abusers may wear masks at first and/or use different identities with the children to utterly confuse them. They would certainly never be stupid enough to take the risk of a child knowing enough about what is going on to betray them to anyone. On top of that, the children are usually so afraid that it would be very rare for one of them to tell about what they have been through. In situations where a child has to return to non-abusive families or carers, the abusers are careful to ensure that the children are not in any way physically marked. This does not mean that they have not suffered. There are a great many ways of severely abusing a child yet leaving no physical outward signs of the abuse on them.

Those born into a family, which has group membership, tend to have a different experience from those who do not live with it on a daily basis. These children are taught at home and within the group and each experience reinforces the other in order to create a child more fully trapped into the whole belief system and more complexly involved in all aspects of the teaching and the religion of the group. These are the children who will, in time, be expected to play a full part in group activities and they will be expected to carry on with the family traditions. From an early age their lives are mapped out by the decisions of the leader of the group and whatever influence their parents may have within the group. They will be expected above all to accept the 'truth' that the group offers and be totally loyal to it.

All pre-school children born into this kind of family setting are generally treated in much the same way at first, regardless of their ultimate pre-determined position and destiny. They are taught to carry out all orders from their parents and superiors both at home and in the group. They are subject to a wide variety of physical control and restraint within the home to teach them obedience and silence. They may be kept tied up for hours, locked in small cupboards, made to eat off the floor and not allowed to wear clothing.

DUNDEE YOUNG WOMEN'S CENTRE

In addition to this, they may be humiliated by being treated like an animal, made to carry out degrading acts on themselves and others and physically and sexually punished in quite extreme ways for the slightest slip up or perceived slip up. By the age of two or three, these children will have learned that they are absolutely powerless and totally dependent on the whims of the adults in their lives. They quickly learn that there is no point in crying, learn to control their emotions and would never dare to throw tantrums like most children.

As well as the physical abuse of the young child, sexual abuse will also have begun. This often begins at home to prepare the child for what is to come in the group setting. Even very young babies are penetrated by objects and fingers and, as they grow older they accept such behaviour as completely normal. For them, it is completely normal. Children before age five will have already taken part in some group ritual activities to some degree and will be very clear as to what is expected of them at any time. Before they are ever presented to the group, they will have been carefully taught about what is expected of them and will suffer the consequences of any failure, perceived or real, on their part. They will have been presented to the group at a very young age for approval and initiation and will have experienced many things that would horrify most adults. To these children, though it may hurt and be very frightening, it becomes very normal to them.

Some children, those who are destined to hold a position of importance in the group, will be very well taught by the age of five. They will be able to talk and understand several spoken group languages and symbols associated with the group. They will be able to write the secret written languages of the group and they will know their place both at home and in the group. They will have been taught about the history of the religion, the importance of silence and absolute loyalty to the family and group and will be very well grounded in the religious teachings. Those children not destined for position in the group or not considered talented enough, are only taught what they need to know and have to do, so that they will do it well. The teaching of the children continues right into adulthood.

Those children destined for high position in a group will suffer in the same way as other children in the beginning as there are some basic things that all children in the group must be able to do. Keeping silent is the main one and accepting sexual activity is a close second. In time however, certainly by age six or seven, they will not be experiencing the same as children with no position in the group at all or a lower position. Depending on what position they are destined for, they will be constantly tested to ensure their endurance, strength and intelligence. These children will be pitted against others, expected to achieve and (in assumption of their genetic dominance), expected to dominate the lower orders. Those who are expected to equal or surpass their parents are carefully taught and trained and any weakness displayed by them is swiftly dealt with in quite extreme fashion. Any found unworthy are quickly weeded out and failure is not tolerated by either the parents or the group and will lead, at best, to being stripped of position and placed in with the children who are 'born to suffer'. These children cannot afford to fail, as the price of failure is too high for them to bear.

Children are brutalised in the group and in turn, many, though not all, begin to behave in a similar fashion to the abusers. Some of the children are not able to cope mentally with the abuse and some seek refuge in dissociation to differing degrees. Some are so unable to cope that they begin to lose control of themselves completely and break down mentally and physically. Some learn to adapt to their lives and find a niche within the group until such time as they either, harmonise with the group and join them wholeheartedly, or find a way to escape from the situation they are in.

Groups differ in how leaders make it to the top and although many groups are generational hierarchies, which means that those at the top pass on the top position to one of their own children. In some groups, there is a constant struggle for position. All children start as equal and are pitted against one another and encouraged and forced into competing with each other. Ultimate position in some groups often comes down to the survival of the strongest, fittest and most brutal throughout childhood and into adulthood. In some groups, the age of majority is twenty-five, though this age varies from group to group.

DUNDEE YOUNG WOMEN'S CENTRE

## Children Getting Out of Ritual Abuse ➢

It is not easy for children to escape from ritual abuse, as they, by themselves do not generally have the resources or the life experience to know that escape is possible or even how to escape. Sometimes, a non-abusive parent or carer suspects or finds out that the child has been abused in some way and the child is removed from the situation. Sometimes, the person taking the child into the abusive situation moves away and the abuse ends. Sometimes, the child moves to live with a different family and the abuse ends. Rarely are the abusers brought to justice, as frequently the child can provide no coherent evidence and it is often a very long time before they can tell about the abuse. At least though, when the abuse ends the child is finally safe.

The only way that a younger child, whose parents are fully involved in a group ever gets out of ritual abuse is through the death of self or parents or through being taken into care. Older children can sometimes escape by running away from home or by behaving in such a way that they are eventually placed in care. Most of the children born into this type of abuse however remain there until they become adults. (This position is not a lot different from children physically or sexually abused in their home.) Even then, as adults they can find it difficult to escape, but some do make it out eventually.

Because it is almost impossible for the children to tell about what is happening to them, it is rare for anyone to intervene, yet children, particularly young children often slip up and do give out some signs that all is not well for them. If more people only had enough awareness of ritual abuse, perhaps it would be possible for more children to be noticed and helped to escape at an earlier age.

Chapter 10

Helping child
survivors of
Ritual Abuse

Chapter 10
## Helping child survivors of Ritual Abuse

### Advice For non-abusive parents and carers

If you think that your child may have been abused, it is important not to keep this to yourself. Talking to other people can help you to work out the reason you are beginning to think the way you are, and may help steer you in the right direction to get some help. It is important not to jump to any conclusions about abuse based on limited knowledge, as children vary so much in how they present and they all react differently to different things in their lives. Sometimes their reactions are nothing to do with having been abused but are to do with something else entirely. It is always better to be as clear as possible about what you are dealing with before you take any action.

If it turns out that your child has been abused, get help sooner rather than later. Try not to quiz your child based on something you have read or jump to conclusions about what type of abuse your child has suffered. Children get very mixed up and confused quite easily and if you have made too many assumptions you can easily put the idea into your child's head that what they suffered was more complex than it really was. Try instead to love and care for your child in a way that is not seeking information, but rather, helping them to recover from the trauma. The child will begin to talk in his or her own time and in his or her own way. Even if what your child says sounds a bit off the planet, remember that sometimes children use fantasy as a means of coping and expressing what they are feeling.

If your child has been apart from you for quite long periods of time, i.e. several days or a few weeks, or you have recently started looking after a child who has lived elsewhere, and you find the child to be very traumatised, something major may have happened to the child. They may have been bullied, frightened or abused in any number of ways and investigative agencies such as the police and social services can help you to get to the bottom of it. Ritual abuse is certainly not the most common form of abuse carried out against children and it takes many different forms. Be open to hearing about anything but keep a firm hold on reality and common sense with anything you may hear.

## The sorts of things that may alert you to the possibility of ritual abuse of your child are:

▸▸ A deep mistrust of everyone.

▸▸ Deep fears about talking about what it is that is frightening or bothering them, even when asked directly.

▸▸ Inability to talk about the past or about their fears.

▸▸ Unexplained or unreasonable fear of things such as crosses, colours, animals, fire, water, or other fairly normal things that most children usually encounter.

▸▸ Unusual fear around particular times of year such as the full moon, Christian or pagan festivals such as Solstices, Easter, Halloween or Christmas and all the trappings and decorations that often accompany these times of year.

▸▸ Unusual and unexplained terror of specific places such as churches, graveyards, warehouses, barns or open spaces.

▸▸ Panic attacks, nightmares, losing time, dissociating, flashbacks and other signs of extreme trauma.

Though you may begin to suspect that your child might have been abused, you cannot know for certain until your child or another witness begins to talk specifically about the abuse. It is always hard for any caring parent to come to terms with the possibility that their child may have been abused but if you are to help the child to recover from this, you must learn how to cope.

For some parents and carers it is even more difficult as, over time, the child begins to disclose the almost unbelievable fact that they were ritually abused. Often this comes out many years after the abuse has stopped and the parent is sometimes able to remember strange behaviour exhibited by their child at the time or soon afterwards. This can lead to a great deal of self-blaming as the parent struggles with guilt at not having noticed the signs of abuse or with their own lack of basic awareness. The main thing that every parent and carer must keep clearly in mind is that the abusers are the only ones to blame in any abuse situation. Self-blaming is understandable but a huge waste of energy that could be focused more productively elsewhere.

Another problem that parents often encounter is their own denial of what is possible. Most people do not believe that ritual abuse happens at all. If they are then faced with their very traumatised child beginning to talk about the unbelievable things that happened to them, their own worldview can begin to crumble and many people understandably take refuge in denial and disbelief. It is easier to believe that a child has only seen a scary movie or has an over active imagination than it is to believe that they may have survived ritual abuse. Having said that, some things that children say are sometimes not only unbelievable, they are downright impossible.

If your child tells you something that you know to be impossible, i.e. 'I saw the man fly across the room', unless you are willing to believe that the man could actually fly, you need to look for another explanation of what the child has said. While the child may hold firmly to this belief, you certainly do not have to. It is possible for young children to believe anything they have been told by adults. It is also relatively easy to trick or persuade children into believing something happened that could not have happened. It does not help the child in the long term to just accept absolutely everything that they say to you. You can accept the fact that currently the child believes what they are saying about what they saw, but somewhere along the line, the child needs to be made aware of the impossibility of some things and helped in looking for an explanation of what they believe they saw.

It is also possible that the child believes what they witnessed because drugs, tricks, illusion or hypnotism were used on them. Certain drugs can cause hallucinations and all it can take, is an abuser suggesting that something is happening to make the child begin to actually see it. Extreme sensory deprivation and terror can also make a child suggestible enough to believe they are seeing something that is not actually happening. While it is horrible to think that any person might deliberately trick and confuse a young child to this extent, a child reporting that they saw a man fly during the episode of abuse for example, would have the effect of reducing the child's credibility to zero. Everything would be instantly dismissed as being too far-fetched and incredible to be believed. This would suit the abusers very well.

It is also possible that the child is coping with the abuse through fantasizing. Sometimes, when young children have no control at all, i.e. they are in an extremely abusive situation, they lose themselves in a world of fantasy. A child in a helpless situation might imagine Superman, for example flying in to rescue them and may hang onto this thought in order to keep the bad things away from them. Though they may talk about their thoughts and memories, some of these may include the fantasies they used to try and cope at the time. Through time and with good quality support and understanding, the child will separate these things out for themselves and eventually recognise what was actually going on for them.

It is not essential to get a child to talk about the graphic details of what happened to help them to heal. Unless the child wants to talk about it in such a way, or if they need to talk to an investigator, it is better to leave them alone. What most children need is to be comforted, reassured and continually told that they are now safe from harm. Essentially, the only people who really need to know the finer details of what actually happened are the child protection practitioners who may work with the child during an investigation. These people are the ones with the skills to find out what the child is trying to say. Parents trying to get information out of the child can sometimes get in the way of investigative procedures. Telling about abuse is never easy and just because a parent may want to know the details, this is no reason to put a child through it. If it does not help the child to talk about something, then why even go there? Surely the wellbeing of the child needs to be the most important consideration?

# Where Angels Fear

Some children do not remember the abuse for a long time and when they do begin to remember, it is very frightening and confusing for them. It is also difficult for parents to begin to understand how the child could possibly have forgotten what happened to them. Yet, it is quite common for severely traumatised children to put terrible memories so far away from themselves that the memories become buried very deeply inside. Only with time, care and sometimes a memory trigger to remind the child of what happened, the memories begin to surface. Sometimes the memories come back slowly over a long period of time and they are almost always very distressing and painful to the child.

Other children never forget but are unable and/or unwilling to talk about what they experienced. The enforced silence and the fear can be too great an obstacle for them to overcome for a long time. Also, as the child gets older and leads a more normal life free from abuse, they realise that what they experienced was wrong and in many ways unbelievable. Sometimes they feel to blame for what happened to them and their perceived part in it and sometimes they find it hard to believe their own memory and begin to take refuge in denial.

Eventually, when children begin to feel safe and have learned to trust the adults now in their lives, some of them do begin to try and talk about what they remember. They normally do so quite tentatively at first and with each new disclosure often come remembered, but real feelings, pain and flashbacks. For days and even weeks after each bit of a disclosure, the child is often stuck in a state of terror and heightened anxiety as they anticipate the 'remembered' threats of the abusers. Only through time do they realise that nothing actually happened to them when they talked about the abuse. Again and again they go through this with each new disclosure. For some it gets easier as they begin to talk, but others continue to feel the same terror each time they disclose something new.

If you suspect that your child has been ritually abused do not try to force them to talk about it. Try to keep an open mind, as you may be wrong in your suspicion of abuse or ritual abuse. Instead, work at building up trust with your child and let them know that you are there to listen to them if they ever want to talk to you about anything. Make time available for your child and encourage them to share their feelings with you when they want to. Try talking through your fears with another adult and write down the reasons that you are beginning to suspect abuse of any kind. You can call the police or social services for advice and information or, if this is too big a step to take, you can call a help-line such as the Samaritans, Childline, the Young Women's Centre or another voluntary agency. Voluntary organisations usually offer a high degree of confidentiality so you can talk through your fears safely.

If your suspicions are realised and your child begins to talk unprompted, about being abused by one or more people, being taken to strange places, people dressing up, animals hurting them, people chanting, torture and child murder and things that sound like rituals being carried out (they will not use the words abuse or ritual), they are possibly talking about ritual abuse and you should consider contacting outside help as quickly as possible. In the case where the child suggests that these things are still happening to them, remove them immediately from the people they are naming or indicating as responsible. It is better to believe the child in the first instance than to take any risks. Investigative agencies will hopefully soon work out if any of the allegations might be true.

## You can help the child by:

Letting your child know that it is safe to talk to you about how they are feeling. Keep telling them that they are now allowed to talk and tell about what happened and that if they want to, they can even tell the police about it.

Letting them stay in control of the process as much as possible by talking when they want, about what they want and to the person they choose to talk to.

Try not to rush to the police or other investigative agencies unless your child is still in danger. Your child may not be ready to do this yet and the process of investigation may frighten them and make them retract what they are saying. Be aware though that the best agency to investigate allegations of abuse is the police and you should avoid too much questioning of your child. By questioning your child you may make the work of the police much harder. Focus instead on making certain that your child is now safe from harm and letting them say the things they want to in their own way and time. Encourage them to talk about how they feel and reassure them that they are doing nothing wrong by telling about things that happened to them. Leave the getting of the details and facts to the child protection practitioners.

Obviously if your child or other children are still at risk, you may need to inform someone in authority quite quickly. Give yourself time to calm down first though so that you will be able to support your child effectively through the investigative process. Waiting an hour or two to give yourself and your child time to think will not generally make any big difference to a child or the investigation. If you must go to the police, if you can, hold back on the less believable aspects of the abuse at first. If you launch into talking about child murders for example, you may well be classed as a nutcase. Try to keep the things you say in terms of, 'I think my child may have been abused', give the reasons you think this and let the police find out the details of it from your child. In most cases the abuse happened many years before and there would be no real proof other than what your child says. Be aware that the less believable and strange things that your child talks about may discredit them.

Find out as much as you can about the subject of abuse rather than jumping to conclusions about it. Find out all you can about trauma and post-traumatic stress and how to help traumatised children. Remember that much of what you read will be theories and the 'one-size fits all' approach may not suit your child. Children, just like adults, are unique individuals with different needs and you may need to shop around to get the most appropriate help for your child.

Do not assume that your doctor will have all the answers for you. Most doctors know nothing about the subject of ritual abuse and therefore nothing about the effects of ritual abuse on individuals. If you are lucky enough to have a doctor who is prepared to learn about it and admit what they do not know, you may be able to get a referral to someone who really can help.

Find out what extra support is out there for your child and let your child know about it and how to access it. It ought to be their choice if they want to have additional support or not.

Avoid, if you can any programme offering to help survivors recover memories. Your child can decide whether or not they want this, as they get older. Memories are often suppressed in survivors for very good reason, i.e. to protect the survivor, they will be recovered quite naturally when, and if, the survivor is more able to cope with them. There is no need to force the process of remembering and it can be dangerous for the survivor as they may not be able to handle knowing it all. There is also the danger that later on there will be an accusation of a therapist implanting false memories in the child. If there is a very good reason for a child needing help to remember something, make sure that it is a fully qualified practitioner who assesses this need. There are often parts of the past that survivors never recall and this does them no harm. Some things really are better forgotten.

Find out what support is out there for you and the others in your family and reach out for it. The more support you are able to get for yourself and your family, the better able you will be to continue to provide support for your child.

Beware of self-proclaimed experts! Some people do have expertise in dealing with trauma and abuse. Some even have expertise in working with ritual abuse survivors. On the other hand, you know your own child better than anyone else and it is your child who has lived through the trauma and needs to develop their own expertise in directing their own healing. No one else can do this for them and people will often help best by providing practical support and being there for the child and the family. On occasions quality psychiatric help can assist with more specific problems such as flashbacks, panic attacks, depression, mental health, eating problems or self-injury. Often though, you will find that your child and yourself gain a great deal of expertise and will end up teaching the practitioners rather than learning very much from them.

## Advice for Friends ➢

Friends can help child survivors a great deal. Even without any understanding at all of what the issues are, other children can be a great comfort to child survivors. Children who have grown up without abuse can teach child survivors just through playing normally and interacting with them. Child friends can teach them how to play, how normal relationships between children work, how to make other friends and how to trust others. Though the young survivor of this type of abuse may at first be quite fearful of other children and adults, they are usually very quick to learn from other children. Children want to fit in and be normal, and being with other children helps them to see how other children behave in different situations.

While it is highly inappropriate to inform other children about any of the facts of the abuse, sometimes it is appropriate to let young friends know that the child is ill or afraid because someone has hurt them. Even young children can accept this simple statement without any other details being provided and can become very gentle and sympathetic as a result of knowing just a little. Letting them know a little can help explain any strange or difficult behaviour in the child which they may have seen and wondered about.

Older people who are friends of the family can help the family out by being supportive of the parents and the child, by finding out about the subject and about abuse in general, by being there for the parents, by lending a listening ear or a shoulder to cry on when needed, by acting as a sounding board and by helping the parents to access additional information and advice. Often the parents are so busy coping with the difficulties that the child is having that they cannot find the time or the energy to seek outside help. Friends can do all this for them more easily as they are more able to be objective and can sift through what information is available and perhaps find the most appropriate help for the family.

Family friends can also help by offering to take any other children in the family out for a while. This will give the children a break away from the house and also allow the parents to spend more one to one time with the abused child. This can help, in that there will be less distractions and more in the way of quality time spent with the child. In addition to this, friends can offer to look after all the children on occasions to give the parents some much-needed respite. Caring for a traumatised child can be very stressful, time consuming and can put a lot of pressure on the whole family. Giving the parents a break from time to time helps them recharge their batteries and do something more normal for a while. Minding the children will also serve the function of letting the abused child know that there are other adults in the world, like their parents or carers, who do not hurt children. It may seem obvious to adults that not every adult is abusive, but for children who have never known anything other than abuse, they still need to learn this. What better way to learn than to spend some time with another non-abusive adult?

Friends can be either a tower of strength or can make things a lot worse. The former kind of friend is definitely preferable. Family friends need to realise that having an abused child in the household often means that the family does not have the same time or inclination to do such things as they used to be able to do, like socialise, chat for hours on the phone or help in an outside crisis. The impact of looking after a young survivor is major and friends help best by being there and not making additional demands on the family. Friends need to do the keeping in touch for a while, try to find out what is most needed by the family and try to offer as much practical help as they can. Friends also need to learn not to expect the same level of support that they maybe used to receive. Adults need to learn to cope with their own problems and put the children first at all times.

Chapter 11
Young People
Involved in
Ritual Abuse

Chapter 11
**Young People Involved in Ritual Abuse**

**As with young children there are several different ways that young people, e.g. teenagers, can become involved in ritual abuse**. Young people being a bit older and more experienced in the world respond differently from younger children and tend not to be as easily taken in to an abusive group situation. With young people, unless they have been born into a group, getting them involved in the activities is done in different, and much more subtle ways.

It is less likely that, with teenagers who have never experienced ritual abuse before, they will end up involved in it at home. Even in the case of their parent marrying into it, it is a great deal harder for the abuser to get older children, who already have the notion of right and wrong firmly set in their minds, to cooperate enough to involve them in an abusive group. Though, in the case of a parent bringing an abusive partner into the home, they may experience some form of abuse and domestic violence, it is very unlikely that they will be used in rituals and group events. There is too much chance that an older child will talk.

Young people who have led lives relatively free from abuse are not quite as easily silenced and controlled as much younger children are. They usually know too much about the real world to be tricked in the same way that younger children are. Teenagers are also not as dependent on the adults in their lives as younger children are and therefore, are much more likely to have outside interests and circles of friends. This sometimes saves them from any approach by members of groups. It is much more likely with young people that they first approach groups and cults, willingly and completely unwittingly, through not knowing exactly what it is they are getting into.

## Young People Born into Ritual Abuse ➤

Young people may already be involved in an abusive group because they were involved as children by their carers or family and have never been rescued from it. For them it may be all they know and to them it is very much a normal way of life. They may never have questioned the lives that they live and they may have very little to compare their life with. From their own perspective, their lives are completely normal. Some of these young people are very controlled by their families and have no easy way of finding out about how other people live. They may have little or no choices at all about getting away or finding any useful information or support for themselves.

Those who have been born into it are already well conditioned not to talk by the time they become teenagers and some may be beginning to act out and rebel outside the home. This is usually put down to typical teenage behaviour. Though many of the signs of abuse are already present in their behaviour, it is rare for anyone to pick up on these signs in a positive way. Young people are a very diverse group and a too quiet and obedient teenager is all but invisible in school while a disruptive and troublesome teenager is often rendered invisible by being excluded from the school. Usually, neither will be noticed as a survivor by anyone. Even constant running away from home, which to many with some awareness would indicate a problem at home, is usually put down to the troubled young person, they are seen as the problem rather than being seen as a troubled young person who has a problem.

By the time young people who have been born into ritual abuse reach their early teens, they will have been involved fully in most of the group rituals. Many will be so indoctrinated in the faith and beliefs of the group that there can be no question of any betrayal of the family and group. They will know by this age what would happen to them if they told anyone, therefore they simply do not tell. Most will be completely unable to trust anyone else, especially adults, and they will have learned that they are totally powerless to resist against those who are stronger than them. These young people are often easy prey to other abusers as they find it almost impossible to say no to anyone, or to defend themselves in any way. They are frequently bullied by other young people and are often very alone and isolated.

Some of these young people, usually those with some status in the group, will have adopted wholeheartedly the ethos of the group to the point of being abusive themselves. They themselves may bully other young people, will not hesitate to abuse their power over younger children and they can be very cruel and sadistic with animals and younger children. They may believe themselves to be superior to others and seem to have a total disregard for the feelings of others. Some of these young people do come to the attention of the authorities as their challenging behaviour begins to impact on those people around them. Unless the root cause of their beliefs and behaviour is discovered and tackled in isolation from the group, these young people often grow up to be the next generation of abusers.

## Young Dabblers ➤

Young people are, by nature, extremely curious and as part of the process of growing up and becoming adults, they can sometimes be rebellious and look to do completely the opposite to their parents. When they discover through other young people, adults they admire or, more and more these days, via the Internet, that there are such interesting things as secret societies, the occult and pornography, some of them begin to express an interest in it. Often they are drawn towards other religions such as paganism, particularly if they have grown up with Christianity. The curiousness and rebellion of youth against the cultural norm, while mostly harmless, can sometimes lead them quite unwittingly along a very dangerous path towards the fringes of abusive groups.

Young people drawn towards the occult, paganism, secret societies and religious cults are already moving in a general direction, which can lead them into trouble. While a great deal of this type of thing is completely harmless to anyone, abusive groups are really well disguised and may appear to be completely harmless at first. Unwittingly, a young person may end up close to the fringes of a group looking to recruit young fresh blood. The young person will be carefully cultivated by members of the group, taught some of the principles of the group and initially pampered and made to feel important. Abusers will begin a brainwashing process, which, as they begin to be able to control the young person more, will increase in intensity. Often there is also heavy use made of drugs to make the young person dependent and more complacent. Gradually the young person becomes drawn in and involved in the fringe activities.

Many young people who get close to the fringe of a group and begin to become involved in criminal activities find this very exciting at first. They feel important and daring and are usually provided with money for the illegal tasks they carry out. Fringe members of the group encourage them in these activities and begin to test them out to see how far they will go. In this way, the group begins to get an idea of the young person's moral code. At the same time, the young person will get teaching in some of the areas they were first interested in. They are taught and shown some of the ideology of such things as Satanism and the occult. One of the first things they will be taught is to fear the power of these things. As risk taking is exciting, the young person not only begins to fear but also becomes desperate to know more.

One of the first things that a group will do, when they have more control is to ensure that the young person is quickly involved in a more serious crime so as to implicate them and thus silence them. The group will make sure that they hold the proof of what the young person did and this can be a useful lever. At first these young people will not be abused by the group but will soon begin to be involved in the abuse of others. They may also be encouraged into other crimes such as trafficking in drugs, stealing vehicles, and distribution of counterfeit money or pornography. The young person may begin to be used for pornography themselves. The young people will not ever know enough about the group at this stage to be able to betray anyone if they ever get caught. Once the group is certain that the young person is properly hooked in and properly silenced, the physical and sexual abuse of them soon begins. By then the young person is totally controlled and silenced by the group and more serious abuse and involvement in rituals becomes possible.

## Vulnerable Young People ➢

Young runaways are very much at risk from all abusers. These young people are already missing from home with no one knowing where they are. Runaways most often rely on theft, prostitution and handouts from others to survive on the streets. It therefore becomes very easy for an adult to pretend to be sympathetic, build up a relationship with the young person and persuade them to go somewhere with them. As they are already reported missing, these young people can easily be taken by an abusive group and can quite simply disappear from the world. As there is rarely any intention of ever releasing these young people, the abusers can do as they please to them from the start. They do not have to bother with the brainwashing or the silencing process as the young person will never have a chance to tell anyway. Survivors of ritual abuse sometimes talk about young runaways being picked up and being used in hardcore pornography and in snuff movies.

Young people in care are also vulnerable to abusive groups. Authority of any kind often disillusions these young people and many feel aggrieved by the very system that was supposed to care for them. As such, they are often socially excluded, may have been abused already and many begin to drift towards crime, drugs and prostitution. Abusers when they get near them, carefully cultivate some of these vulnerable young people and through a pretence of caring about them, can begin to pull the young person into the fringes of the group. At first, this often suits the young person very well. Many young people in care, in Scotland at least, are thrust abruptly out of care and left to fend for themselves at the age of sixteen. These young people are extremely vulnerable and become easy prey for those abusers who want to recruit young people for their own uses.

In care itself the young people can be abused by the care workers if the workers are so inclined. For young people who have been in long-term care, already they have often been pillar to post within the system and they seldom have any one person that they have been able to build and sustain a good relationship with. It is, unfortunately, very easy for those workers who are involved in an abusive group to strike up a relationship with the young person and begin to recruit them for the group. The fact that so many of these young people crave love and affection, makes it easier for abusers to cultivate them and to be able to abuse them.

## Young people getting out ➢

The most common way that a young person manages to get out of a group situation is through running away from home. Repeatedly running away from home is a common theme mentioned by adult survivors and many attempt it at quite a young age. Realistically, running away, as a tactic of escaping the group, cannot be managed and maintained until the young person is actually old enough to take care of themselves, or old enough to ask someone for help. Even when many of them reach the legal age for leaving home, few actually succeed in doing so. Often they are too traumatised by their experiences to get away from the group and stay safely away. Few know how to survive alone and few would know where to get help, even if they could overcome their distrust of adults long enough to think about asking anyone for help. The older the young person gets, the greater the control that the group exerts over them. In many ways, it actually gets harder to get out of the abusive situation the older the survivor becomes.

Some young people do succeed in getting away from the abuse. Sometimes the authorities find them, and if they have created enough of a nuisance of themselves, they may be placed in local authority care rather than being sent home again. This is more likely the more out of control they are. There will still be some contact with their family, as the survivor is unlikely to tell anyone about the abuse. At least, though while in care, they are distanced a bit from the family and to some degree protected from the most extreme forms of the abuse. This can often give them the chance they need to find a permanent way out. It can let them see a different way of life and may give them a better idea of how they can live free of their family.

Others run away from home and such is their mistrust and fear that they manage not to be found by anyone. These young people often survive on the streets rather than live at home or tell on the abusers. Though they are very vulnerable on the streets, some actually prefer it to living with their families. Sometimes on the street they find their way to a safe house and are provided with help and support. Some of them go 'willingly' into a life of prostitution as a means of survival and consider it to be a better life than where they came from. Some are picked up by and move in with adults who abuse them but in a more gentle way that the survivor considers not as bad as where they came from. Others, in time, sort themselves out and eventually get themselves a home and a life free from abuse.

Some young people, who have not grown up with such abuse but are drawn into it, realise their mistake quickly enough and succeed in getting free from it. If they have a non-abusive family they can find a way to contact, they can quickly access help and have a safe place to go. Many of these young people have become so brainwashed and silenced by the group that even with the support of a good family, they often find it very difficult to betray the group and talk about their experiences for a very long time. Their families are often completely in the dark and are bewildered as to what has happened to the young person. In time, some young people are able to talk about it and get help to deal with their traumatic experiences.

# Chapter 12
# Helping
# Young Survivors

Chapter 12
## Helping Young Survivors

**Young people who have had any dealings with groups of abusers need a lot of support to come to terms with what has happened to them.** If rituals and brainwashing have been part of the abuse, they will find it very hard to talk or tell about what occurred in any coherent manner. With abuse, it cannot ever be said that any one persons abuse is worse than another persons experience, as things that happen to any individual are relevant only to them. Having said that, a person who has grown up with abuse has often found ways of coping with the abuse and it is to some extent all very normal to them. In many ways the coping mechanisms that they have learned in order to survive the abuse continue to function and can help them to find ways of living without the abuse.

For a young person who has never been abused before to suddenly find himself or herself in the position of extreme horror and powerlessness is a sudden shock to their whole sense of being and identity. Such a shock can be utterly devastating and can render a young person completely unable to cope in any way. Some of these young people may be so traumatised that they need long-term professional help. I have known cases in which the young person has become completely catatonic for a period of time, as their brain has simply not been able to take in any more. While this is a normal human reaction to what has happened to them, it can be very frightening for others to deal with and understandably many parents and carers panic.

Traumatised young people can be extremely difficult to live and work with. Their behaviour can become extreme and very challenging indeed. They may act abusively towards others. They may exhibit criminal behaviour. They may cause harm to themselves through drugs, drink or self-injury. They may withdraw into themselves and refuse to communicate with anyone. Being an adolescent is difficult enough at the best of times, but being an adolescent who has been severely abused can be much more difficult. While it is perfectly understandable that the young people are reacting strongly, it is also difficult to help them to help themselves while all this is going on.

Perhaps the best way to begin to reach out to a young person who has been severely traumatised is to find someone who can take all the time in the world to begin to build a relationship of equality and trust with them. This may not be easy at first, as adults may have to step in from time to time and take control of the young person to prevent further harm to the young person and to others. Some kinds of behaviour just cannot be permitted to happen and if the young person cannot control himself or herself, then someone else needs to do it for them. This authority person is usually the parent or carer and as a result, they are seldom the people best suited to building a trusting and equal relationship. If someone else can do so however, it can, in time, work wonders for the young person.

A friend of the family, a youth worker or a worker from a voluntary organisation can be approached for help in this matter. Providing the person is trustworthy, honest and genuinely caring of the young person, they can begin to make some headway with the survivor. Though it will take time for a relationship to build, it is worth taking this time, as it will pay off longer term. It also helps a lot if this person does not report everything said by the young person back to the parents or carers but keeps a high degree of confidentiality with the young person.

With the young runaways, because they are so mistrustful of adults, it can be difficult to reach them with offers of help. Sometimes the police pick up these young people and, either take them back home if they know their identity, or into care if they refuse to let the police know anything about themselves and no missing person report is filed for them. In care, if they stay long enough, there is a chance that they may eventually relax enough to begin the process of beginning to trust someone. If the young person looks old enough to possibly be a young adult or close to it, the police sometimes leave them alone. Occasionally, police officers take the time to build a relationship with young street kids and this can be invaluable in terms of the young person realising that some adults, even those working with the police can be okay.

Although leaving young people living on the street can seem like an almost uncaring thing to do, in many ways, the survivor is safer on the street than at home. At least if they are lucky enough to have a police officer keeping a friendly eye on them, the young person can benefit a great deal from this. Street workers, from a variety of organisations, can also be invaluable in helping young survivors who have run away from home make safe links and safe contacts with responsible and caring adults. In time, the young person may begin to trust, talk and begin to get appropriate help.

## For non-abusive parents and carers ➢

Parents and carers can suffer great stress and anxiety through trying to care for an abused young person. Unlike a younger child, who will throw tantrums, but can be controlled and comforted with a cuddle, young people are usually too big and far too sophisticated for this sort of thing. Parents and carers often have to endure screaming matches, trashed bedrooms, running away, dangerous behaviours, mental health problems, suicidal youngsters and a great deal more. Unlike most parents who may occasionally have to deal with some of these things in ordinary teenagers, they have to endure this hour after hour, day after day. While they may be very understanding, if they know about the extent of the abuse, understanding in itself, is simply not enough to get through each day with their sanity intact.

Even the most loving and understanding parent or carer in the world would find it hard to cope alone with such a distressed and traumatised young person. Add to that if the parent or carer has other children to care for, the difficulty of looking after the needs of the non-abused children alongside the needs of a traumatised young person. Sometimes too, as the young person feels let down by adults, yet feels safe enough to vent their frustration and anger on parents or carers, these poor people face the brunt of all the anger and distress. While it is a positive thing that the young person can express their anger at all, it is extremely hard for non-abusive carers to deal with and accept these outbursts. While in time this anger will become focused more appropriately, in the beginning, parents and carers have to find ways of coping with it.

Sometimes parents end up in the position of listening to disclosures. If there is a good relationship between the parent and young person, despite outbursts and tantrums, the young person sometimes feels safe enough to begin talking. Often a great many of these disclosures come immediately after outbursts. While it is good that the young person is beginning to talk, the things that the young person talks about can be very difficult for a parent or carer to hear. A lot of what the young survivor says will be unbelievable. A lot will be horrible to hear. All of it will be unacceptable to a loving parent. Parents and carers have to deal with this without any specialised training or support and frequently with no awareness of the issues at all. The fact that so many manage is a testament to their love and willingness to care for the young person. Parents and carers in this position can benefit a lot by finding some support for themselves in order to continue to cope.

Parents and carers in this position need to get all the help they can to support the whole family, not just the abused young person. Many turn to the psychiatric services or social services for help but often feel let down by the response, or lack of response they get. Parents often need to battle long and hard with agencies and keep on demanding practical and emotional support for themselves as well as help for the traumatised young person. So few people in all the different professions understand, believe or are prepared to work with survivors of ritual abuse that getting help for the young survivor is seldom easy.

Parents and carers have to become extremely demanding and be prepared to keep up the pressure until they get the help they need and deserve. They also need to begin to recognise their own expertise with their own child and not be taken in by people who, by virtue of their position, assume that they know better. Just because someone is a consultant, a social worker or a doctor does not mean that they understand ritual abuse or the particular difficulties of the family. They are not living with it, never have lived with it and probably never will live with it.

Chapter 13
# Adults involved
# in Ritual Abuse

Chapter 13
## Adults involved in Ritual Abuse

**There are generally two distinct types of adults involved in ritual abuse groups**. Firstly, there are the adults who want to be there and have a clear choice in what they are doing. These are the people who can come and go at will, gain both financially and personally from the activities of the group and are involved in getting pleasure out of the situation. They are often people who have been born into a position of power in the group and fully embrace all aspects of it. It would not suit these people to leave the group or allow others to leave. Amongst this group are also those people who have actively sought involvement in ritual abuse and joined a group as an adult. Other adults are associated on the fringes and work at keeping the groups going because it suits their own self-interest.

Then there are the adults, often born into it or dragged in while young, that do not want to be there and who have no choice at all in what is going on. These are the ones who have no power at all, are controlled by the group and who suffer in every way imaginable so that others may gain in wealth, position and power. The first types of people are of course the abusers and the second are the abused. It is the only the second type of person that we are concerned with in this book, as some of them are the survivors that we encounter. The only interest in the abusers is in how to expose them and put a stop to their activities for good.

The first type of adults, the abusers, generally have far too much to gain by staying in the group to ever want to consider leaving it. These adults are the ones who can indulge themselves to any degree of depravity that their imaginations can think up and are hardly likely to want to give up their secret and illegal pleasures. Some of them will also be aware of how difficult leaving can be and of the price they would pay for trying to leave. They may once have been children on the receiving end of abuse who finally decided it was better to join the abusers and be like them rather than always being on the receiving end of abuse.

The abused, not surprisingly, are the ones most desperate to get out of the group. Many of them reach the stage of thinking that the only way to survive is to escape. Often escalating abuse as a particular planned event draws near, causes their desperation. Sometimes the abusers have simply gone too far and pushed someone over the edge so that the need to get away surpasses all previous fears and all control. Other times they believe they have nothing else to lose as the worst thing possible has already happened to them. Occasionally, they believe they are going to die, or be killed, and have nothing more to lose by trying to escape. For whatever reason adult survivors begin to try and make the break away from the group, these are the people who become the survivors we work with and support.

## Adults Born into a Group ➤

As indicated previously, survivors, when born into this type of abusive family, find it very hard to get out even, or sometimes especially, when they become adults. Sometimes this is because they are so completely controlled that they have no opportunity to get out of the group. They have nowhere to go, no means of independent living and no money or knowledge of how to get money or accommodation. Often they do not have the life skills to know how to live independently in this world, as they have never been allowed to develop these skills. Often they have been deliberately denied any opportunities to learn so that they must remain dependent on the group for basic survival.

Adults in this position find it extremely difficult to get to any outside help, and if they manage to run at all they are usually quickly found and taken back. Often as they are legally adults, people on the outside do not realise that they are unable to function in the world as most adults do. For example, they may not be capable of making any choices for themselves, as they have never been allowed to do so before. When presented with a choice, they are completely unable to cope with the concept of this. These survivors are not stupid, often they are far from it, it is just that some things are completely outwith their own experience of life.

Some adults in this position are so resigned to being in the group that they have accepted it as a way of life. They can see no other way to live having never known anything else. Some resign themselves so completely that they cease to resist at all and just do exactly as is required of them by the group. Others, despite the increased suffering caused by resistance, continue to resist and co-operate no more than they are forced to by the abusers. In many ways, this can suit the abusers, as the group members often like to have some form of resistance, providing there is no disruption to the general operation of the group activities. Resistance becomes an exciting and stimulating challenge for abusers and frequently leads the group members into greater extremes of abuse, which they can then declare to be the fault of the survivor for their continuing resistance.

Adult survivors do succeed in escaping from the group on occasions but the many years of torture and abuse makes it extremely hard for them to survive without support. They have to find a way to get away in the first place, manage to resist the impulses to return to the group and avoid being found by the group. They also need to be able to learn very quickly how to live in a very different culture from which they have been used to all their lives.

## Marriage and Partners ➢

Abusers often seek out vulnerable people (usually women) such as survivors of abuse, single parents, people with drug or drink problems or people with learning difficulties. There is a certain tendency to seek out people with young children in particular so that they can, in time, get easy access to the children. On finding vulnerable adults, they take the time to build a relationship with the person and, over time, may get married or become partners.

In the beginning, the abuser carefully cultivates the relationship and puts on a great show of respectability and reliability. Once they manage to move in with the person and gain some power, they begin to gradually change. As in cases of domestic abuse, the abusers work slowly and carefully at breaking down all resistance until they eventually have total control over the individuals. They isolate, brainwash and totally dominate individuals emotionally at first, then they move on gradually to carrying out physical and sexual abuse. The control and the abuse are gradually increased with the parent and any children until it has become quite extreme. At the same time, the abuser ensures through isolation, threats and brainwashing that the silence is maintained by all.

When the abuser has control over the individuals concerned, the involvement of other abusers begins. This may happen initially by bringing friends home and expecting cooperation from the partner in allowing the friends to abuse them. This heralds the beginning of involving the adult individual in ritual abuse. The adult survivor soon becomes completely overpowered by the constant abuse and this leaves the door open to begin the abuse of any young children. Sometimes, the parent does not know at first that their children are being abused and often they are made to cooperate with the abusers by threats against the children if the parent does not comply with any demands. The parent, sometimes believing that they are protecting their children, and being too afraid of the abusers to stop their own abuse, begins to comply with any and all demands.

By the time the parent discovers that the children are also being abused, they are so thoroughly involved and totally controlled that they find it very difficult to leave the situation. In a similar way to domestic abuse, they have nowhere to go, are too afraid to leave, are brainwashed into accepting the abuse and have no financial independence. Though some parents, on discovering that their children are being abused, do manage to get away, others do not. Some people just give up and learn to accept it and some, in time, actually end up embracing it as a way of life.

Those who do succeed in getting away can risk losing their children to the abuser. This tends to happen if they have married, allowed the children to be adopted by the partner or have any shared children. As the abusers usually appear to be upright citizens, applications for access are usually granted. Sometimes the adult survivors are so traumatised by their experience that they become quite ill after getting away and this is a golden opportunity for abusers to step in and declare themselves better suited to looking after all of the children. If at this point the adult survivor tries to tell about the abuse, they are simply seen as mentally ill or vindictive and the unbelievable things they are saying, especially about an upright citizen, makes them sound mad.

## Adults Dragged into Ritual Abuse ➢

Some adults are dragged into ritual abuse in a number of ways. Some vagrants for example are enticed by the offer of drugs, alcohol or a warm bed for the night. Vagrants tend not to be missed or accounted for in the same way as other people and are thus very vulnerable to being preyed upon. Although abusers often prefer young people and children, survivors report that occasionally an adult  vagrant is dragged in to the group to be used in a ritual murder. These people seldom escape from this situation and even if they did, they would have little or no credibility if they ever tried to talk about their experience.

 When the group is seeking to recruit members, they sometimes turn to those on the fringes of the group. As these people are already indicating an interest in such things as child pornography and child abuse, they clearly have something in common with those already involved in the group, and as such, some are open to being recruited by a group. Others are initially involved at the fringes and coerced or even blackmailed into taking part in increasing group activities and levels of abuse, these people are gradually drawn into the group until they are full and active members.

These types of people will rarely be privy to any information, which they could use against group members and will rarely rise in position, power or status within the group. Although these people are getting what they want from the group in terms of free access to children and involvement in torturing and sexually assaulting others, the group controls and gets a lot out of them. They become the willing congregation and in time have to share some of their resources with the group. Many do this willingly as they get such huge personal benefits from the group with no real risk to themselves.

The groups deliberately recruit people with high position, status and money in outside society. Not only does this provide some regular finance for the group but it can also provide someone who may be in a position to help the group in a number of ways. For example, if a group member has access to a large isolated house, the group will welcome the opportunities provided by having access to a good venue. Alternatively, if the group member owns or edits a newspaper, they can very easily discount any reference to ritual abuse and ridicule any survivors who try to speak out about their experiences.

People who become interested in the occult, paganism and anything to do with the left hand path can also become interested in the activities of groups. They may actively seek to join a group and become involved in it without knowing at first that the group is abusive. They are kept completely in the dark at first about the abusive side of things but in time; begin to become involved in other activities. Sometimes they are coerced through the use of drugs or alcohol to become involved in the sexual activities. They may not even know at first that not everyone participating in the activities is willing. As they are encouraged into more and more activities through their new faith, their morality is gradually broken down until they are hooked into the whole thing.

## Adults Getting Out ➢

While many would assume that it must be much easier for adults to escape from an abusive group than it is for children or young people, this is not always necessarily the case. Adults who have been involved since birth are often so conditioned and controlled that, for them, it is almost impossible to get out. For other adults they may feel they cannot leave because of blackmail, loyalty, the abusers having control of a child of theirs, or because they fear the retribution of the group.

The abusive adults rarely want to leave the group as they get so much out of it but many adult survivors have been involved, through the use of force in the abuse of others and often believe themselves to be abusers also. The group deliberately sets out to blur the distinction between the abuser and the abused and are often so successful at achieving this aim, that many survivors believe themselves to be abusers and therefore completely to blame for all that has happened to themselves and others. These survivors are often so guilt ridden by what they think they have done that even if they do escape, they find it extremely difficult to seek support or talk about what really went on in the group.

There are a great many myths surrounding ritual abuse and one of these myths is that adult survivors are potentially dangerous people who will report everything about their supporters back to the group. It is surprising the amount of people who actually believe this. While there are people involved in groups who will constantly seek to disrupt, and will deliberately do things to create a climate of fear and distrust of survivors, genuine survivors who are trying to break away from a group will not do this. The real difficulty is in knowing who is a genuine survivor and who is actually an active group member who is out to make it even more difficult for future survivors to get help.

Adult survivors, when they do start to break away from the group, are faced with such tremendous difficulties that getting clear away, at the first attempt, is almost impossible. Leaving an abusive relationship of any kind is rarely a single event but is more usually a process, which happens over a long period of time. Often survivors have to try many different tactics to get away and stay away, until they finally find the one that begins to work for them. Those who are lucky enough to find a person or an agency to support them through the process of leaving the abusive situation are the ones who tend to finally make it.

Possibly the most important part of the process of leaving such abuse is finding a way to become properly accounted for in the outside world. Once survivors have found a niche in the world outside and they have found someone who will ask awkward questions if they ever disappear, they are much more likely to be left alone by the group. The last thing a secret and abusive group of people ever wants is anything at all that will draw any attention to them. Survivors are generally not believed at all when they talk about the abuse, therefore the group is relatively safe in the unlikely event that a survivor ever says anything. If, however, anything starts to happen to the survivor, it begins to have the effect of validating their stories, however bizarre they seem to be.

Although it is very difficult, adult survivors can and do escape from groups. They also learn to find a way to live safely in the world. People often think that once survivors have managed to escape from abuse, they will now be okay and will be able to just get on with their lives without any more problems. Unfortunately, this is rarely the case, especially for ritual abuse survivors. It is often only when all the abuse finally ends that the survivor begins to experience the debilitating effects of post-trauma. This is the time they possibly need the most support. They really need all their support to continue and may even need more support than they had previously.

Chapter 14
Living with
Ritual Abuse
Survivors

## Chapter 14
## Living with Ritual Abuse Survivors

**It is extremely hard for survivors who have escaped from a group to come to terms with their abuse and very difficult for them to learn to live in a world where the rules they grew up with have all changed dramatically.** It is also extremely hard for those who live with survivors and share their lives to learn how best to help them recover. Ritual abuse survivors are understandably very traumatised by their experiences and many will be quite ill and struggling with life for quite a long period of time. Their problems will be as varied as any individual experience can be and may include mental health problems, self-injury, difficulties with trust and problems with making and maintaining relationships. While the survivor is learning to cope with their new life, those who are close to them and sharing their lives with them are also learning to cope with change and a great deal of new knowledge they possibly would rather never have discovered.

Many survivors come to live with non-abusive people in a variety of ways. Some survivors, as children or even as young adults, are adopted or fostered. For a variety of reasons, they have been taken into care and out of the situation of abuse and are unable to live independent lives. Other older survivors, find friends to share a home with, some find partners and some go into supported accommodation. Family life can change for all time and it can be very challenging when a ritual abuse survivor joins the family in whatever way, but it can also be a rewarding and fast learning experience for all involved in the process.

Survivors of abuse are no harder to live with than anyone else, but as their life experiences have been so different to what most people regard as normal, adjusting to new life can take a very long time. Also, the people that survivors come to live with usually do not know at first that the newcomer has been abused. It can take many years for survivors to begin to disclose any abuse and even longer to disclose the ritual side of the abuse. As a result, it can be many years before people know that ritual abuse is the underlying issue for the person.

Most people have never encountered ritual abuse before and they can find it very difficult to understand what has happened, or know how best to help the survivor. Even once they know that they are living with a survivor of ritual abuse, they often do not know what to do or say for the best. Most people learn the hard way and make many mistakes as they go along. Many struggle to come to terms with the fact that someone they have come to know and care about has suffered in such a terrible way.

Even for those people with very good awareness of the issues, there can be difficulties in adjusting to the situation. It is one thing to have awareness of a subject but another matter to become very close to and emotionally involved with, someone who has been directly affected by the same subject. Learning about different individuals and learning how to live with individuals can be difficult at the best of times but if you add abuse and trauma to the equation then the difficulties can increase dramatically.

This chapter is an attempt to prepare people in advance for the joy of living with and sharing their lives with a survivor of this kind. It is also an attempt to provide some tips on how to cope.

## Adoptive Parents and Carers ➤

When you adopt a ritual abuse survivor of any age it will quickly become apparent to you that your adopted child is a little bit different from other children. Though you may know little or nothing abou  your child's background, the signs of trauma will soon begin to appear once they are removed from the abuse. These signs are often hidden while the child is still being abused as the child has usually learned ways of coping with the abuse. Once the abuse has been stopped and the child is in a place of safety and beginning to learn to trust a little, the child is then able to begin the recovery process.

Part of this process is thinking about and remembering the abuse. Many survivors do not actually forget about it, they simply are so busy surviving each day that they are not able to think clearly. Sometimes when they are finally safe, they are constantly flooded with the memories over and over again as their brain tries to assimilate and make sense of the painful memories.

The memories they get can be intrusive to the point that the survivor constantly relives the abuse over and over again. Sometimes these memories are so powerful that the survivor believes the abuse to actually be happening. They see the place it happened, see the people, smell the smells, hear the sounds and feel the pain. All of this is extremely distressing to the survivor and it is difficult for parents to understand what is going on, particularly if they have no prior knowledge that abuse ever happened.

The first thing that a parent may notice is that the survivor is in a constant state of hyper-vigilance. They are alert to everything, watchful, sometimes very still and often appear very anxious for no apparent reason. They may startle easily or freeze at every little noise, sudden movement or when people enter a room. Survivors, even in sleep, may keep this up and waken sharply and suddenly at the slightest noise or movement. When they waken from sleep, they are wide-awake and some may even spring to their feet and look ready to run.

Often the parent will notice strange reactions such as cowering away when someone passes too close, hiding in cupboards or under the bed, extreme fear of common objects and appearing sometimes to switch off to everything around them. There can be other things such as unusual responses to pain e.g. laughing rather than crying, getting physically shaky at certain times of day or year, rocking, head-banging, repeating the same sentence or word over and over again and many other such things. Most parents, even if they do not know that their child or young person has been abused, will certainly notice and consider some of these things to be unusual and not quite normal behaviour.

Once the penny drops and the survivor trusts someone enough to start to disclose the abuse, most parents can quickly recognise that what they are seeing are the signs of trauma. Even when this is recognised, it is difficult to know how to live with it and how best to help. The parent is the main person that needs to learn how to care for the survivor, as even for those survivors who get therapy or medical help, the parent is the person closest to and interacting most often with the survivor.

## Partners ➤

Many people get involved in relationships with survivors of ritual abuse without knowing at first that this is the case. Then again, abuse is not usually the first thing that a person would ever choose to tell someone they were beginning to go out with. Sometimes further down the line, as the survivor grows to trust their partner more, they may begin to talk and gently test the waters about raising the complex issue of abuse. Often ritual abuse survivors, for very good reason, tend to just talk about being an abuse survivor at first. In time, this can change and the survivor may begin to let their partner know more about their background.

For the partner, once they know a little bit about what the survivor has experienced in the past, it can help them to understand more about some of the things that go on between them. Realising that the reason a partner has difficulty in trusting people has nothing to do with any lack in either person, but is more to do with how one of them grew up, can actually help the two people in the relationship work better together. Finally knowing the reason that a partner has cut off totally from their own family and does not want anyone, especially the children, to even know any of the family can clarify a very important matter, which may not have been understood before. For people who have grown up with loving and caring parents and have kept a good relationship full of regular visits and family events, it can be very hard to understand without any explanation why anyone would disown their own family.

Other things can also become much clearer once the survivor reaches the stage of disclosing even a little to their partner. Things such as having strange phobias, fear of the dark, refusal to enter a church, refusal to seek medical attention even when needed, difficulties in intimacy and many more things can begin to be better understood. Some survivors may begin to talk a little about their beliefs and again this can be very revealing for the partner and help them to understand the reason behind such things as their partner not celebrating Christmas or Easter, or having difficulty with these particular times.

Sometimes one partner begins to suspect that the other has some difficulties and begins to notice problems such as the occasional panic attack, flashback or periods of dissociation. Depending on the awareness level of the partner who begins to notice, they may suspect abuse to be in the background of their partner. Partnership is about sharing both the good times and the bad and even without knowing any of the details of abuse, a good partner can offer great support. Any person caring about another is a really good starting place but the partner can take this further by offering to get advice and finding places that will provide support to the survivor.

Many of the difficulties arising in partnerships come out of a lack of knowledge, awareness and misunderstanding. This is no different from any partnership. Sometimes though, with survivors of ritual abuse, there can be additional problems around talking about difficult issues and feelings. Many survivors react to stress and difficult emotions by dissociating and a total avoidance of the problem. The survivor often interprets emotions such as frustration, upset or anger as signs of danger. It is usual for partners in any relationship, to feel and express their emotions but when these expressions of emotions are then misinterpreted by the survivor and lead to panic and fear, it becomes difficult to even have a discussion round the issue without the survivor misinterpreting what is going on.

While the reactions of the survivor may be understandable, the partner can find it increasingly difficult to make any sense of what is actually going on. In an ideal relationship, in which one or even both people are survivors of abuse, both would be able to access support and advice from outside the home. Also, in an ideal set up, both people would be able to talk openly and honestly about what the problem is and how they can deal with it. Unfortunately, few people have an ideal relationship and none live in an ideal world. Most people just muddle along as best they can.

Survivors of ritual abuse can and do have relationships the same as anyone else. They are no less able to love and care about others than anyone else. Though many of them have had a turbulent start in life, they can get over this and are as normal as anyone else. Like everyone else, they may, from time to time, experience stress and need to find ways of dealing with this. Sometimes they and their partners have to work hard at avoiding conflict at first, then finding ways of facing up to and dealing with any difficulties.

Some survivors have memory triggers, which can push them into having flashbacks at any time, but a sensitive and caring partner can help the survivor deal with this. One of the most difficult areas can often be round intimacy. For some survivors, though they want to be intimate with their partner, each time they try, it triggers a powerful and awful memory of the abuse. The partner needs to quickly recognise when this has happened, immediately stop what they are doing and try to remind the survivor of where they are now and whom they are with. Though this can be difficult for both parties, dealing with it rather than avoiding it is the best way forward.

Intimacy can also lead to problems if the survivor has trouble in saying no or expressing an opinion on things they do not like. It is common for ritual abuse survivors to have difficulty in refusing advances, particularly sexual advances. Many of them just go along with the wishes of others and try to please people in the way they have been taught. Sometimes, partners are horrified to discover that something has happened between them that the survivor did not want to happen. A simple thing, such as allowing the survivor to take control and initiate all intimate contact at first can be very successful in dealing with this. Talking about what has happened, without any blame attached to the subject can also help a lot.

One of the things that often affects partners of ritual abuse survivors is the anger they can feel towards the abusers. Often, because they are so close to the survivor, they can see the damage that has been caused in a way that others cannot and when they begin to hear some of the detail of the abuse, they can get very angry on behalf of their partner. Often they cannot express this anger to their partner as sometimes the survivor misinterprets this and thinks that their partner is angry with them. Still the anger is well justified and it is better to be safely expressed rather than bottled up. The best way of dealing with this type of feeling is to find a safe person outside of the relationship to let off steam with, preferably with the consent of the survivor.

At the end of the day, partners of survivors do need to recognise that while they may feel very angry and frustrated, the survivor is the one who was abused in the first place. How the survivor feels about this may not be the same as how the partner feels about it. Survivors may not feel anger towards the abusers even though they would be well justified in feeling this. Often partners find this difficult to understand and expect the survivor to be as angry as they are. Sometimes too, survivors get annoyed at a partner for expressing anger about something that was personal to the survivor. Both need to be able to feel what they feel and allow each other to express their own feelings in as safe a way as possible without affecting the other.

## Friends ➢

People make friends all the time and usually at the beginning of any friendship little or nothing is known about each other's background. Only through time, building trust and the growth of the friendship do people begin to share information about their lives with each other. With some friends we share much more than with others and everyone has their own level of how much they are willing to share and with whom. All this is perfectly normal and most people have grown up learning about the dynamics of friendship and how it all works.

For survivors of ritual abuse, this can be very different. Many will not have formed friendships while young. Rather, it is more likely that they have learned to avoid and mistrust other people. Many will have learned while still quite young that they have to depend on their own resources to survive in the world. They may have learned that friendship is a dangerous thing, through such things as being set up by the group and provided with a 'friend' who subsequently betrays them. Though not all survivors will have difficulties with friendships, many will until they learn more about it.

It can take a long time for many survivors to move towards a friendship with anyone, and when they finally do, many are quite cautious and fearful at first. Often the first friends they make are through the people they live with or the support agencies that help them, but in time as they begin to spread their wings a bit, their experience of friendship grows. Because many survivors do not trust or make friends very easily, those friendships they do make are very important to them. This can put a lot of pressure on the friends.

As trust is so vital to survivors, any breach of trust by a friend, no matter how little it may seem, is a major problem for a survivor. This can be difficult for many people to understand as they often think that the matter is trivial. But for a person who has repeatedly been betrayed, to finally place their trust in someone else, and then find that the person has breached this trust, this is absolutely devastating. Survivors can be very literal in what they say and often do not have real life experience of the outside world. They only know what they have learned to date and this can easily make for misunderstandings and confusion.

One of the worst breaches of trust any friend can make is to tell anyone anything about the survivor's background. Even to let someone else know that they are a survivor is a huge breach of trust. While people who are not survivors may not understand this very well, it is a very private matter to the survivors themselves. It takes a great deal of courage for a survivor to share this type of information with anyone at all and unless a survivor says to share it with others, it should always be kept strictly confidential.

Sometimes when survivors feel they can trust a friend, they may begin to talk a bit about their experiences. This can be hard on someone who has absolutely no experience of abuse. Rather than pretending that it does not bother them to hear this, friends are better to be completely up front about how they feel about this. Some people can cope and even consider it an honour that the survivor trusts them enough to share personal information but other people simply cannot bear to hear about the terrible things that have happened to other people. Friends need to be able to be completely truthful with each other and if they do not want to listen supportively or cannot bear to hear it, they can help the survivor by finding quality support services for them.

By the same token, friends should not pry into each other's lives. On occasions when a person finds out that their friend is a survivor, they are so curious about it that they start to ask too many prying questions. This can make life hard for the survivor as it may throw them back into painful memories. Many will struggle to answer questions even though it makes life difficult for them. It is better to always ask first if it is okay to ask questions, but try to remember that most survivors of abuse find it very difficult to say no to anyone. While asking questions directly often enables survivor to speak, this should only happen in order to help a survivor in some way. People may need to know some things in order to help but there is a great deal that they do not need to know about. Survivors will tell things when and if they choose to.

A friendship with a ritual abuse survivor can be just the same as a friendship with anyone else. They are just as reliable, honest and trustworthy as anyone else. Many people make the mistake with survivors, once they discover that the person is a survivor, of then putting every problem encountered in the friendship down to the person's background. While occasionally this may be true, it is not always and it can begin to feel like blaming the survivor for everything that goes wrong in the friendship. It takes two people to build a friendship, two to maintain it and two to create problems and destroy it. It cannot always be the survivor who is solely to blame in a difficult or problematic friendship.

Sometimes, survivors make friends with people who are supportive of them. In time, the survivor gets stronger and no longer needs the support side of this friendship. Some people find the fact that the survivor is no longer dependent on them for support very hard to deal with. Rather than being happy that the survivor is moving on and getting stronger and becoming more able to sustain a more equal type of friendship, they cannot give up the power of being in the position of supporter or carer. Often this leads to disputes as the survivor begins to challenge this position. Often the supportive friend believes that the survivor is too damaged or subjective to make decisions for themselves and the survivor begins to struggle for independence. Sometimes it becomes very similar to a parent and young adult conflict.

People must remember that in order to learn and grow, adults and young people must be allowed the freedom to learn some things for themselves. Even if on occasions this means that they will make a mistake and get hurt, they must be allowed to try different things out. People can often become so overprotective of survivors that they unintentionally restrict and hamper their personal freedom and development. Friends are friends, not parents or carers and must always try to remember this. Sometimes this is hard as so often survivors bring out the caring side of people who then feel the need to look after the survivor. Remember, the survivors survived the worst things imaginable; they can survive without any one individual.

The best thing a friend can do for a survivor is be a real friend to them. Treat a friend who is a survivor like any other friends. Be honest, give respect and lend a listening ear if you can. With most survivors you will get the same in return. Most survivors are excellent listeners and extremely supportive of other people. Share your troubles with them too. Sometimes other peoples problems are more easy to deal with than your own and listening to a friends problems can distract a survivor from their own worries for a short time.

Chapter 15
Helping
Survivors of
Ritual Abuse

Chapter 15
**Helping Survivors
of Ritual Abuse**

**Anyone at all can help a survivor
if they are inclined to help. No
special training or special skills
are needed and just being a
human being goes a long way.**
Specialised help is available in
some areas if the survivor needs or wants it, but ordinary people can do a
lot themselves. There are many books on the subject if people want to
know more, but the survivor is the real expert and most will teach if people
are willing to listen. Listed below are a few points, which might help in
understanding some of the common issues for survivors.

⇨ **Trust** is a major issue for all survivors of abuse, but for a survivor
of ritual abuse it is fairly certain they will have absolutely none at first. They
will have learned from their experiences in the group to trust no one at all.
Some will never have known what it is like to trust another person and
some will have had all trust systematically destroyed by the abuse.
Survivors are often put in the position of getting to know someone and
thinking that they can trust that person, then the person deliberately betrays
them. This can happen many times throughout the abuse until they are
too afraid to trust anyone at all. However this does not mean that they can
never learn to trust. Even survivors who have lived with ritual abuse all
their lives can eventually learn to trust someone but it can be a long process.

# Where Angels Fear

Firstly people need to realise that the survivor has no reason whatsoever to trust them. In fact, such is their life experience that they have the opposite. They have a multitude of reasons not to trust anyone. Many people, especially professionals such as people who work in health services or the police make the mistake of thinking that because of their position everyone will automatically trust them. This is not the case. Many survivors have been deliberately made to mistrust professionals so that they are rendered unable to approach them for help. This mistrust is easily done. All the abusers have to do is let the survivor know that some of them work in the police, social work or health. Even when this is a lie, the survivor has no way of knowing this and will be fearful of anyone working in the same agency. In addition to this the abusers may repeatedly tell survivors such things as the police work for them. This can be easily 'proven' by the police bringing young runaways home again.

It can take many years for a survivor to begin to trust someone. The person has to constantly prove themselves to the survivor as trustworthy and even then, the survivor may wait for the inevitable betrayal that they expect. It is much easier for survivors to believe that they will be let down and be prepared for it than it is to place their trust in another individual and then be betrayed. If that is their only experience of life then anything different is difficult for them to imagine.

In order to begin to build trust with a ritual abuse survivor of any age it is best to begin by never making a promise you cannot keep. People, who do not think far enough ahead, often without thinking it through, make promises. Yet no one can tell at the beginning of any relationship between individuals what sort of thing might be disclosed through time or what issues may come up in the future. It is far better never to make any promises at all, than to make one that later you find yourself unable to keep. If you break a promise you also break trust.

Being truthful and honest with a survivor at all times is a fundamental part of building trust between individuals. While there may be some things that people are unable to tell a survivor for some reason, it is important not to tell any lies. It is far better to let the survivor know that some things cannot be revealed and give the reason, if possible than, it is to tell a lie. Better still, just steer clear of anything that cannot be talked about. If you lie to a survivor and they find out about it, you have again broken their trust. Survivors are used to being told lies, they expect it from everybody and are used to it. If other people then tell them lies this reinforces the messages of the abusers.

Without trust it is almost impossible to build a sustainable relationship with anyone. Without trust it is almost impossible to comfort or care for someone. Without trust relationships are tenuous and easily broken. In many ways trust is the first building brick towards beginning to heal. Trust is taken for granted by many people but can never be taken for granted by survivors. It is something that has to be earned and learned and takes a long time to achieve. It only takes seconds to destroy it for all time. All anyone really needs to do to prove themselves to be trustworthy is to actually be trustworthy consistantly over time.

⇨ **Fear** is a constant companion for survivors. They have frequently lived with it for so long that they cannot imagine life without it. Even long after survivors are removed from the abuse, the fear remains with them. They may fear people, animals, objects, places or any number of tangible things because their experiences of these things have been terrifying. There may also be less tangible fears such as the fear of going to sleep, fear that something is going to happen to them, fear that the abusers will know everything they say, or any number of other fears.

Though people sometimes find it difficult to understand the fears of these survivors, the fear is very real and debilitating for the survivor. It is also based on their own experiences. These fears need to be expressed and talked through. They need to be understood, not just by the survivor, but also by those who live with and care for the survivor. There are always good reasons for the fears and they should never be dismissed as silly or unreal. Even though a supporter may not see or understand the fears, survivors feel them. Gentle and constant reassurance that the survivor is safe now, acknowledging the fears of the survivor and helping them explore their feelings and where these feelings are coming from can all really help.

Survivors almost universally feel a strong sense of **guilt**. The abusers will have constantly impressed this guilt upon them, and the vast majority of survivors will blame themselves even before they blame the abusers.

Some of this is due to the way the abusers manipulate survivors into believing that they were the cause of the things that happened. This can be done by making the survivor believe that they have erred and therefore needed to be punished, making them believe that the abuse is designed to teach them to be stronger and better people or making them believe that what happened was right but they were flawed in some way for not liking it. Abusers will even point out the unflawed people (abusers generally) who are enjoying the proceedings as the proof of what they say.

Most ritually abused survivors feel tremendous guilt because other people, generally very small people, have been hurt and abused also. Offering survivors no win choices in regards to the abuse of children increases this guilt. An example of this might be telling a survivor to choose the next child to be abused. If the survivor refuses to choose anyone, the abusers choose three children and go on to hurt them badly. The next time the choice is given, if the survivor refuses to comply even more children get hurt. Very quickly, survivors begin to choose a child. This can be moved on quite rapidly to the survivor being told to hurt one child. The choice then becomes of the survivor believing that they will cause far less suffering to a child than the abusers will.

The other thing that can happen is that the survivor is made to hurt others or be badly hurt themselves. Given that most of these survivors learn the cost of non-compliance at a very early age, many do not question this. Though few like what is happening, they are absolutely powerless in this situation and none of the choices are real. These survivors are not abusers, though often they feel as though they are. When they escape from the group they are ridden with guilt about their acts. They find it very difficult to see that they really had no choices in the situation and that the abusers were the ones who were making all the decisions.

In addition to this, survivors are often sexually touched and stimulated in such a way that their body begins to respond sexually or they have an orgasm. They have no control over this at all and frequently feel confused and betrayed by their own body. The human body is designed to react to certain stimuli and these abusers know them all. The abusers will not hesitate to point out to the survivor that they enjoyed what happened.

They will point to any physical reaction of the body that indicates arousal and insist that the survivor is indicating their willingness. These bodily reactions confuse and dismay survivors, many are unaware of the biology of it all.

While it is difficult to help a survivor to let go of the guilt feelings, it is possible to start the process of beginning to counter such negative and self-destructive thoughts and feelings. Telling a survivor repeatedly that they are not to blame, the abusers were, is a great start. Listening to a survivor talk and asking them to explain why they think they are to blame or what they are to blame for can help in the understanding of it all. Usually it takes a very long time before survivors are able to stop blaming themselves and often an even longer time before they are ready to place any of the blame where it really belongs.

⇨ **Trying to leave a safe home** is also symptomatic behaviour of survivors from time to time. Even though they know that they are perfectly safe, such is their conditioning to return to the abusers that they find it extremely hard to resist this. On these occasions survivors are very much at risk. Often it is clear that they do not want to leave, but there is such a growing feeling inside them that they feel compelled to leave the safe home and return to the abusers. Often they become restless, fearful and begin to believe that they, for some reason, cannot stay where they are. Such is the compulsion that some survivors do return to abuse.

The conditioning of the survivors to return at set times is part and parcel of their experiences. The abusers reinforce this compulsion by ordering survivors to be somewhere at a certain time, then making it impossible for the survivor to get there. The survivor is then severely punished for not being where they were meant to be. Then there is the belief in the 'faith'. Survivors may believe that they, must attend certain events and not to go will lead to dire consequences for them and others. On top of that, survivors are sometimes hypnotized and post hypnotic suggestion is implanted in the survivor.

Even for several years after leaving the situation of abuse some survivors find it difficult not to return. If they do return, not only will they be abused, but also every compulsion and belief will be reinforced in them and make it harder for them the next time. They may return to the safe house again, particularly if they are accounted for and any long-term disappearance will be noted and reported, but the need to return again will be even stronger the next time.

Survivors are usually very clear about saying that they do not **want** to go, but they **need** to go. Often older survivors will find ways of thwarting the compulsion to return by making it too hard to go. They will arrange for people to visit them. Arrange for people to phone them and some will even get someone to lock them in the house and take away the keys so that they cannot leave the house. Younger survivors can be prevented from leaving by their parents and carers but often, safe adults cannot understand what is actually going on. It is difficult for most people to understand how someone who has made it to safety can actually feel the need to go back into danger.

Survivors, like many other people, find it difficult to face things they find hard to deal with, and sometimes the compulsion to run away from everything is strong. This is especially true for anyone who has developed the instinct to run away as a means of coping with life. Running away has become such an instinctive thing to do that they are often up and running before anyone even has time to think.

Often too, when survivors are not coping with how they are living now, they begin to feel that they must return to their original home. Their argument is often along the lines of, at least at home they knew the rules, knew where they stood and in this world they do not know anything. This is often due to their lack of understanding of how this culture works. They often have no idea of what is expected of them or of how to behave. They find the actions or inactions of others extremely confusing, the lack of structure and rules distressing and end up feeling totally unsafe. Bear in mind that they have come from a position of being totally controlled and knowing exactly where they stood in the group to living in a world that they perceive as chaos.

Providing structure and rules can help a lot, particularly with younger survivors. This gives the survivor a sense of at least knowing what the rules are and it can make them feel safer. The rules can include not going out without saying where they are going, taking a mobile phone with them, saying a time they will be home, phoning in if delayed and other such safety rules.

While this will help with younger survivors, many older survivors have no parent figure to help with this. There is an assumption that when people reach the chronological age of adulthood, they become responsible for themselves. This sometimes works against survivors who are completely unable to keep themselves safe. Sometimes these survivors are completely unable to stand up to the abusers and the compulsions to return to the groups and so the abuse continues. With the help of friends, and their agreement during the better times, things such as the safety rules above can be put in place to keep them safe.

⇨ **Suicidal thoughts and compulsions** can plague a survivor who has reached safety. Often, even although they do not actually want to die, they feel a terrible compulsion to do so. While some do end up feeling so bad that they become suicidal of their own accord, the group has programmed others to have these thoughts. Survivors can end up believing that they must die because they have betrayed the group. The price of betrayal is death, or so they have been taught, and sometimes the waiting is too much for them. Many survivors firmly believe that the group can reach them anywhere and they have been taught that the group is all-powerful and all knowing and will kill them if they leave. The belief can then shift; if they take charge and kill themselves, they deprive the abusers of doing it.

Sometimes survivors have also been taught that to talk will mean their death. Any attempt to talk then quickly leads them to feelings of suicide or waiting for death to come. The other thing that can happen is the hypnotism of survivors, to try to take their own lives at given times. Many believe that they are destined to die at a preordained time and place and it may even be written in the 'holy' book of the group. When this date arrives, the fear and compulsion becomes extreme and unbearable. Survivors need to be gently reassured and comforted through these periods. They also need to be kept safe from themselves as well as the group and people in their lives can often help by trying to understand, helping the survivor to understand and making sure that they are not left alone until these feelings and thoughts pass.

It is only if the suicidal feelings are really about feeling so bad that they constantly want to die that professional help might be needed. Most survivors are survivors rather than victims because they have an exceedingly strong will to live. They have lived through some of the most horrendous abuse imaginable and are unlikely to really want to give up on life when they have reached safety. Although survivors may talk about wanting to die, this does not necessarily mean that they intend suicide. While it is important to keep a close eye on them and let them talk about what they are feeling, there is seldom a need to rush to save them. Most survivors of ritual abuse are looking for ways to try and live, not for ways to try and die.

⇨ **Self-injury** is often a strategy that people use in order to find ways of coping with their lives. It can take many different forms and can include such things as cutting, burning, head-banging, hair-pulling, swallowing pills or objects, inserting objects into self and any other variety of things that can cause harm to self. People who self injure can be incredibly creative about finding ways to hurt themselves.

Though much of this is outwith the experience of most people, injuring self as a means of coping is common in people who are very stressed or traumatised. Just because someone uses self-injury it does not mean that they are mentally ill or trying to kill themselves. More often than not, it means that they are trying to stay in control of their lives, finding ways to deal with their inner pain and suffering or expressing themselves in a way that works for them. Self-injury rarely leads to death and many survivors, through time, find other ways to cope.

Self-injury is more likely to be a problem for the people who care about the survivor. It is never pleasant to see someone you care about hurt even if they have caused the hurt to themselves. It is also very difficult for most people to begin to understand what is going on and most people find themselves pretty horrified to find out that someone can inflict pain and damage upon themselves. Although most survivors attempt to hide what they are doing to themselves, when you live in close proximity, it cannot always be easily hidden.

People close to survivors who use self-injury can actually do quite a lot to help once they get over the initial shock of discovery. They can help by asking the survivor about it in a non-judgemental manner. Sometimes people who self-injure have a lot of insight into what they are doing and the reasons behind it, but others can be as bewildered as their supporters. Either way, it can never do much harm to encourage a survivor to talk it through with someone rather than having to deal with it alone. Sometimes when survivors start to talk about it they can gain much more insight and begin to explore different ways of dealing with their feelings and reducing the harm to themselves. The other useful thing that can happen through talking about it is that people close to the survivor may begin to understand better and become more able to be supportive of the survivor.

It is often useful to encourage survivors who use self-injury to try to consider their safety before, during and after self-injuring. By this I mean making sure that they use clean blades if they cut, being careful where they hurt themselves e.g. avoiding bleach near the eyes and cleaning and caring for any wounds afterwards. Most people who use self-injury never attend a doctor or nurse afterwards if they can prevent it; this is particularly true of ritual abuse survivors who often fear these medical professionals. This is all the more reason for encouraging them to stay as safe as possible when they feel the need to self-injure. Try hard not to condemn the self-injury or demand that it stop immediately. What is most likely to happen in this event is that the survivor will just try harder to hide it. At least if it is out in the open, you are more likely to know the full extent of it.

Encourage the survivor to take control for themselves rather than attempting to impose control on them. They can be encouraged to make up a first aid kit particular to their own needs. They can be helped to look for other ways of coping with their feelings, or of expressing themselves. They can be encouraged to make changes for themselves over time. Survivors of abuse have already been in situations in which they have been powerless and have had no control over their bodies and they usually need to be allowed to take back power and control for themselves. At the end of the day their body and mind belong to them and they do have the right to treat their body as they please even if this means hurting themselves.

⇨ **Hypnotism** can be an issue for some ritual abuse survivors and those who care for them. Often survivors have been hypnotised by the abusers as part of the abuse to make them more compliant. This often starts in childhood and continues as long as they are involved in the group. People who have been hypnotised many times seem to become much more open to suggestion and further hypnosis. On occasions, post hypnotic suggestions are made to survivors and this can cause them problems for years afterwards. Post hypnotic suggestions can include going to particular places at specific times, trying to leave a safe place and becoming trance like and very suggestible for periods of time.

It can be distressing and confusing for survivors to be unaware of what is happening and of what they are doing. On occasions, they find that they have placed themselves in danger without knowing how it happened or they can lose time and be completely unaware of what has been going on. Seldom will a survivor who is carrying out a post hypnotic suggestion remember anything about what has happened to them. Often it is the people around them who are able to tell them what they were doing. It is rare that these people understand what is happening either, as they have no explanation at all for the strange behaviour of the survivor.

Before anyone can begin to understand and help, they first have to try to find out what the survivor is experiencing. Seldom do people recognise at first that post hypnotic suggestions are behind some behaviours. This is rarely the first thing that anyone would think as generally people have little experience of these things. Rather, people usually assume that the survivor is suffering from flashbacks or is in a state of dissociation. Sometimes this will actually be the case, but not always. As the survivor has no memory of what is going on, it can help them a lot if the people around them can help them figure it out.

**There are signs that supporters and carers can watch out for that might point them in the direction of considering hypnosis as a possibility.**

## The following are some indicators:

▸▸ Survivor appears to be asleep, and cannot be wakened.

▸▸ Survivor suddenly falls asleep even when standing, and if standing actually falls over and appears to instantly be asleep.

▸▸ Survivor appears to be unaware of anything about them. They do not respond to those around them, stare into space, and appear to be in a trance.

▸▸ Survivor behaves in a robotic like manner, i.e. speaks only when asked to speak, answers in a monotone, answers only yes or no to questions, carries out any commands without question.

▸▸ Survivor tries to leave the home without any explanation, at an odd time and in a strange trance-like manner.

These are a few simple indicators that the survivor may have slipped into a hypnotic state. Although there can be other explanations of what might be happening, hypnotic states in survivors who have grown up with this are common in the early days after escaping abuse. It can be a good idea to ask the survivor if hypnotism was used in their group, as some may be aware of whether or not it was a common occurrence. If it was used on others, perhaps it was also a feature for them.

As with all problems that survivors experience, people around them want to help but are often afraid that they make the problem worse. It has to be said that a truly caring person may occasionally make a mistake but they are unlikely to make things worse through trying to help as long as they constantly check with the survivor about what they are doing and why they are doing it. Survivors who have problems through being hypnotised in the past, if they are open to the idea of going to consult a properly qualified hypnotist, the problems encountered can be, in time, resolved. Unfortunately, most survivors will not consider hypnotic treatments at all. This is totally understandable given that hypnosis has been part of their abusive experience.

Often helpers have to try and find other solutions. One of the things which can work really well, and certainly does no harm, even if it does not actually help, is counting the survivor slowly back to the here and now. This involves simply telling the survivor that we are going to count slowly from one to five and by the time we reach the number five, the survivor will be fully awake and alert. Speaking softly, say we are at number one and are going to move up to number two. When number two is arrived at, tell them that they are moving towards being more awake. Then say we are at number two and are now moving towards number three and again point out that with each progressive number we reach there will be a gradual move towards alertness and awakening. This is continued until we reach number five and tell the survivor that they are now awake and alert. It usually works!

Sometimes, when the survivor appears to be in a very deep trance state, there is a need to repeat the process more than once or increase the number of counted steps. Variations on this method can be such things as using the vision of climbing up a number of steps to reach wakefulness. Beginning with, 'we are standing on the bottom step where you are asleep but we are going to climb up the five steps to becoming fully awake. Again the survivor can be talked up each progressive step until they are alert and awake again. This method can also occasionally work with flashbacks in bringing the survivor out of the past and back into the present time.

Other things that can help a survivor with hypnotism problems is always telling the survivor what has happened while they have been 'absent'. Talking about the problem and acknowledging it for what it is can help the survivor begin to take some control back for themselves. Let them know that their mind and body belong to them and they can be in control of the things in their own lives. Talk to them about whatever helps pull them out of the trance and encourage them to do it for themselves, i.e. if counting works for them then they can start to do it for themselves at the first sign of 'fading away'. Encourage survivors to try to notice what it is that triggers any episodes and encourage them to work out where the triggers have come from.

⇨ **Drugs** can sometimes be a problem for survivors if they have been used as part of the abuse. Drugs are commonly used by the abusers to control and confuse survivors to the extent that sometimes survivors can be addicted to the drugs. When such survivors escape the abuse, they may need medical help to withdraw from the drugs. Obviously it helps to know exactly what they are addicted to, and a blood test, if they can stand it, can sometimes reveal this. When survivors are addicted to a drug, they need additional support. Not only do they need help as survivors, but also they need understanding and support through dealing with their addiction. Unlike most people addicted to drugs, they have never made the choice to take 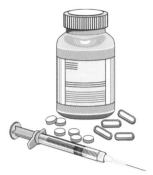 the drug in the first place. Similar to other people addicted to a drug, coming off the drug can be so painful that relapses are frequent and can happen particularly when stressed.

The other problem that survivors can face through being forced to take drugs is that many of their memories can be very confused. Hallucinogenic drugs for example can so alter the minds perceptions that it is difficult for them to know the difference between reality and fantasy. This means that the survivor finds it difficult to distinguish which parts of a memory are real and which are not. Supporters can help by allowing and encouraging survivors to talk. In time, most survivors will begin to make some sense of the memories for themselves. They may for example remember being given a drug by pill, needle or through a drink. This can help them begin to understand why it is that suddenly the memory they have is awful but relatively straightforward at first then becomes quite bizarre after they are drugged.

A less common problem for a survivor who has frequently been drugged is the fact that some may develop a very high tolerance for some drugs and an over-sensitivity to others. Occasionally, when some survivors are given medication by doctors to help them through a crisis, the medication is wholly inadequate for their needs. Usually it takes many weeks before the doctor realises that low doses of a particular medication has no effect at all. Meanwhile the survivor continues to suffer. Alternatively, some survivors are provided with a low dose medication and have an extremely bad reaction to it as their bodies have somehow become sensitised to it. It may be better for survivors to avoid medication, if they can manage without it. It is better, in the long run, to deal with their feelings. However there are occasions when medication may be of some help in the short-term. It is best that survivors work out for themselves how they are affected by different medications. One way of doing this is to encourage survivors to keep a careful note of their reactions to different medications. The next step is to make sure that they try to let their doctor know about how they are affected.

⇨ **Dissociation** is one of the coping mechanisms commonly used by survivors of abuse to survive with their minds still intact. Most survivors learn instinctively in early childhood how to shut themselves off from the awful things that are happening to them. Dissociation can become so instinctive for some people that survivors continue to dissociate long after the abuse ends. Dissociation can vary from shutting down on feelings, drifting away in the mind, switching off all thought processes for a period of time to constantly splitting self into different personalities. As a general rule, the more severe the abuse experienced, and the longer it goes on, the greater the level of dissociation that may be experienced by survivors.

Dissociation is a normal human reaction to trauma, not a mental illness. Even the more extreme form of dissociation, which results in the formation of numerous personalities, or inside people, created to cope with different aspects of the abuse, is a perfectly logical and normal reaction to a series of abnormal and abusive events. A child who can no longer cope with what is happening, in their mind tries to switch off, but of course the child is still physically present. A creative child can shield itself to some degree by creating within itself another child (in its mind) to take their place. This creation becomes the one who copes with the abuse. This process can be so successful that the child survivor and ultimately the adult learn to use it over and over again. They cannot physically escape from the abuse, but they can escape mentally by constantly replacing and recreating themselves.

While this can be a creative and perfectly reasonable way of coping with abuse while living with it, it can sometimes become a problem for survivors once they manage to escape from the abuse. Survivors can face difficulties such as losing periods of time. This happens because of a lack of communication and awareness between the different personalities that make up the survivor. As one personality takes over from another, for whatever reason, neither knows about the existence of the other. When the first one returns, a period of time has passed but they have no idea what has happened while they have been gone. This leads to loss of time and a great deal of confusion which most survivors become very adept at covering up.

Another difficulty can be constant internal conflict as each personality has a different opinion, wants something different or simply wants to be the presenting person in the world. This can make survivors feel as though they are going a bit mad as they often hear voices and arguments going on inside their heads. Some survivors in trying to cope with this, seek medical help, sometimes and are diagnosed as suffering from schizophrenia or other medical condition and put on medication. This does not always help the survivor.

Perhaps one of the biggest difficulties for survivors who dissociate to the extent of forming different personalities in Britain, is the complete failure of the medical practitioners to listen properly to survivors and accept the existence of multiple personalities and indeed ritual abuse. Constantly survivors are faced with such a complete denial of their personal experiences and failure to listen to them that they cease to approach the medical profession for help. Constantly survivors are categorised, labelled and medicated. The medical profession attempts to pigeonhole survivors into theories and models, which cannot possibly accommodate them.

Listening properly, observing and feeding back observations to the survivor can often be very effective in helping a survivor who dissociates. Anyone prepared to spend a bit of time with a survivor who dissociates, can help the survivor to fill in the time gaps by simply telling the survivor what went on while they were 'missing'. There is no need to be an expert. The survivor is the real expert and will, in time, sort things out for themselves. Dissociation, even to the degree of having multiple personalities, is not an illness or a disorder; it is a very orderly and logical response to the disorder that the survivor has experienced in their life. The fact that the survivor actually survived the abuse means that they can survive the surviving and healing processes.

Everyone always wants someone else to do the fixing for them. When in trouble, we all search frantically for an expert who knows how to fix things. Unfortunately, though experienced practitioners can help in guiding survivors and providing reassurance and information, the reality is, at the end of the day, each person has to do the fixing of themselves, for themselves. This should never mean that they are on their own and should not be fully supported and helped along the way. The journey towards healing is a long and painful journey and it can make a tremendous difference to a survivor to have someone walking beside them for at least part of the way.

⇨ **Flashbacks** are intrusive and painful memories, which can flood into the mind of a survivor at any time. The survivor has no control over these memories and they can come at any time and in different ways. Sometimes it can be like a video playing repeatedly in the mind or can be sudden flashes of parts of a memory. Sometimes the memories are so powerful that they can completely overwhelm and incapacitate the survivor. It may feel like the events are actually happening over and over again and sometimes the survivor can see, hear, taste, smell and even feel the event as though it is happening now. They can lose the sense quite rapidly of where they really are, whom they are with and what time it is. Sometimes they believe themselves to be in the time and place they were in at the time of the abuse.

Flashbacks can be triggered by any number of things that remind the survivor of the event. They can occur on the dates that things originally happened even for many years afterwards. They can happen if the survivor is reminded by a smell, a word or phrase, by seeing someone that reminds them of the abuse, by trying to talk about the abuse or through hearing something that triggers a memory. Flashbacks can also occur out of the blue for no apparent reason known to the survivor.

It can be very distressing for survivors to find themselves constantly overwhelmed by these memories and it can cause them to become quite ill or feel incapable of doing anything. Many try to avoid situations which cause flashbacks and while this may work in the short term, avoiding situations begins to reduce the things that survivors can do. This may lead to greater isolation and a reduction in independence. As practically anything can trigger the flashbacks, it is far better to find a way of coping and dealing with them rather than trying to avoid the triggers.

In many ways, flashbacks are the minds way of trying to sort out and make sense of the traumatic events, which have happened. Flashbacks are perfectly normal and anyone who has experienced a trauma of any kind can experience them. Most ordinary memories are processed and filed away by the brain and can be recalled without difficulty. Some traumatic events remain as hot spots and the brain seems to be unable to process them in the same way. These are the sorts of memories that come back as flashbacks. The trick in getting them to stop is for the survivor to find a way of coping while it is happening and then learning how to process the memories.

Different things work for different people. Some survivors find that by talking through the memories with someone, the memories begin to stop coming back in such an intrusive fashion. While talking about it, it can get worse for a while but then it begins to settle down gradually. Other survivors find that drawing or writing or even a combination of the two can begin to make a difference for them. Others find that by discovering a means of grounding themselves in the present time, they can begin to think about and sort through what is happening for them. Grounding can be about having a safe person to call, learning breathing exercises, listening to music, relaxation or a multitude of other things that survivors can do to keep themselves in the here and now.

Whatever method works for a survivor is the one to use. Everybody is different in this and something that works for one person may not work for another and it takes time for survivors to find out what works best for them. Some survivors say that it was not anything particular that they did, it was the passing of time itself coupled with being away from the abuse that made the real difference for them in the end. Though different things work for different people, being in a safe place, having support, and the passage of time, always seem to be part of the process of healing.

Other people can help survivors a great deal when they are having flashbacks. Sometimes it helps just to be there in a caring way. Talking to the survivor, reminding them of where they are, and whom they are with, can also help. Listening to the survivor when they want to talk, or finding someone they can safely talk to is also important. If the survivor trusts another person, they may benefit a lot from being held and hugged in a gentle manner and constantly reassured by the person that they are safe now and nothing bad is happening to them. This only works if the survivor wants this and is comfortable with it. Children especially can be helped a lot just by being safely and gently held for long periods of time.

⇨ **Panic attacks** can be experienced at different times and in different places. Sometimes they occur on leaving the safety of the home or when going into shops or other places. The survivor often feels intense fear, the heart races, the breathing quickens and they can feel as though they are about to die. This feeling is so awful that the survivor may begin to avoid doing the things that they feel started the attack. This can mean that they stop going out, stop going shopping and stop going anywhere associated with the feelings of panic. If left to develop further, the survivor can quickly become very isolated, and limited in what they can do, or where they can go. They may even end up completely housebound.

At the very first indication that the survivor is having one of these attacks people round them can help by offering reassurance, encouraging the survivor to continue doing everything they normally do, getting them to talk through what is happening and staying with them until they have calmed down. Though it can be terrifying for the survivor to face something such as going out when it causes a panic attack, offering to go with them can provide a sense of security enough to lessen the feelings each time. Try not to force a survivor to do something that causes extremes of fear and panic but at the same time, being firm, and insisting they try a small bit, can save them from developing the symptons of agoraphobia.

⇨ **Sleeping problems** are very common with ritual abuse survivors. Abusers often carry out their attacks and ritual events throughout the night and nighttime seldom feels safe to a survivor. Often they have endured sleep deprivation for long periods of time, have been awakened repeatedly and abused as children and fear that if they fall asleep the abusers can get to them in some sort of a 'magical' way.  Survivors seldom have a very good sleep pattern to start with and the many years of disturbed sleep have often set a pattern of sleeping for brief periods, sudden wakefulness, staying vigilant while asleep and sleepwalking.

Some survivors have been taught that there is something called an astral plane that all people can drift to when they are asleep. As children they are encouraged to believe this and end up believing that the abusers can always reach them on this level. Whether or not any of it is actually true is neither here nor there, what is important is that the survivor believes it to be true and therefore becomes too afraid to sleep. Just telling survivors that they are wrong or mistaken will not help allay this type of belief. While it is okay to let a survivor know that their belief may not be widely shared, no one has the right to tell another person that their beliefs are wrong. It is better to tackle this by finding ways that the survivor can stay, and feel safe while asleep.

Suggestions such as sleeping during the day rather than at night for a while can help if the survivor is in the position of being able to try this. Other things might include setting an alarm clock so that they control their wakening times, gathering things around them that give them a sense of safety and security i.e. a teddy, dream-catcher, security blanket or clothing worn by someone they trust. Someone they have learned to trust sitting by them while they sleep can also help at first. A young child can be cuddled to sleep by a safe parent and a partner can stay awake until the survivor has settled down. The main thing to remember is that nothing should ever be done or tried without first getting the consent of the survivor. Only they can know what makes them feel better or worse.

Patterns of sleep can, in time, improve as the survivor begins to feel safer. Unfortunately, nightmares often begin to intrude and can constantly disrupt the sleep pattern again and again. Encouraging the survivor to talk or write about the nightmares may begin to help with this, and in time, they will lessen in intensity. On occasions, a brief course of sleeping pills may help the survivor to cope but they are never a good long-term solution to this type of sleep problem. What they can do though is give the survivor a break from the disruption and a proper sleep for a day or two.

⇨ **Sleepwalking** is another problem that some survivors and their carers have to learn to cope with. Some survivors are so distressed while asleep that it manifests in episodes of getting up and wandering about, leaving the home while still asleep or repeated patterns of behaviour over and over again i.e. things such as going through the motions of washing, hiding in corners or pacing around the room. All of this can occur while still fast asleep.

While sleepwalking is mostly harmless, though sometimes exhausting, severe forms of it can be very dangerous, for example, such things as leaving the home during the night and while asleep can, and do, sometimes, lead to survivors being attacked by abusers or even being hit by a car. The survivor can be so caught up in what their subconscious is projecting that they may become completely unaware of any dangers around them. Even milder forms of sleepwalking can lead to survivors falling down stairs, switching electrical equipment on and leaving it on, or simply having repeated accidents because they are not fully aware of where they are and what they are doing while asleep.

Some survivors go to great lengths to try and stay safe once they know that they sleepwalk. They have been known to lock themselves in the house, tie themselves to the bed and set alarms to waken more often. Sometimes even these precautions fail to keep them safe as somewhere in the subconscious they know such things as where they have hidden the house key, how to untie themselves and they even, in their sleep, can switch the alarm clock off before it rings. This can be very frustrating for survivors as it is almost as though they are constantly fighting against themselves.

People who live with, and support, survivors can help a lot by simply staying with the survivor while they sleep, if this is appropriate, encouraging them to talk about what is going on for them and helping the survivor look at practical ways of staying safe. Supporters and carers can also help the survivor to access professional help, which may be able to help them unravel the causes of the sleepwalking episodes. There are many myths around the issue of sleepwalking, and people living with survivors who do this, often get very worried in case they do the wrong thing and make things much worse for the survivor. A good example of this is the fear regarding wakening the survivor.

A simple rule of thumb with sleepwalkers is that if they are walking into danger, wakening them is surely better than allowing them to get hurt. If possible, gently guide the sleepwalker back to bed while softly reassuring them who you are, where they are and telling them that they are safe. If they waken, they may be very frightened and confused but again just keep talking softly and gently to them until they are calm enough to go back to their bed. You cannot do any real damage to a sleepwalker by being gentle, caring and understanding. The real damage has already been done by the abusers and compared to that, wakening someone is really not a big deal.

⇨ **The beliefs held** by a survivor, particularly a survivor who has grown up with ritual abuse, can be very different from the usual beliefs held by most people in this society. Sometimes, on escaping the abuse, survivors lose a great deal. They may lose their home, their family, their friends, their religion and all the things that most people take for granted in life. Their beliefs and faith maybe all they have left to cling to as their whole life collapses around them and everything changes. They are often rapidly swept along into a strange culture they do not know or understand in any way. All that they knew previously is gone.

Many people think that escaping from an abusive situation means that everything will now be okay for the survivor. This is far from the reality of the survivor. Not only does the survivor now have to deal with the effects of post trauma and the effects of losing everything that they ever knew, but they also have to learn how to live in a completely different type of world. Often they are in deep shock and are very afraid of what will happen now. They may fear that the abusers will find them and come and get them. Though the abuse was awful, sometimes the familiar feels safer for people.

Survivors who have grown up being taught a religious faith, and have come to believe in that faith, do not suddenly decide not to believe in it any more. They may have escaped from the abusive group and may disagree with many of the actual practises of the group, but they do not necessarily stop believing in the actual religion or the deity associated with it. They believe that they may have seen actual proof of this deity so many times with their own eyes that they can do nothing other than believe in its existence. Also, for many, being abused in the name of a deity makes the deity seem all too real. For them it was very real indeed.

A survivor cannot be expected to simply shrug off years of training and conditioning. Neither can they be expected to shed their whole belief system just because they are out of the abusive group. Many survivors cling to their beliefs for a very long time after escaping. Until they can work out for themselves where they stand and have had the time to learn about the beliefs of others and compare them, they need, quite often to believe in something.

Some need to believe as a way of explaining what happened to them. It is easier to believe that the abuse and torture was for a reason or a higher purpose, than to believe that your own family would do the things they did for personal satisfaction. People need reasons and explanations for the things that they experience, even if these explanations and reasons fly in the face of normal societies beliefs or even logic. Many cling to the belief that their parents really loved them and were only doing the things they did for the child's own good and to make them a better person. It is sometimes better for some people to believe this, rather than believe they were not loved at all by their parents. Some people are just not ready to deal with thinking that all they grew up with may have been lies. In time, survivors, just like everyone else, form their own beliefs and question their beliefs for themselves.

If there are **children** living in the household that the survivor moves into, parents and carers need to make sure that the children are still adequately cared for and are not affected by any of the issues surrounding the survivor. Much depends on the age of the survivor in this. A child survivor entering a household will need a great deal of time, attention and support for a very long time. If there are already children in the family, they may feel jealous, left out or distressed by any challenging or strange behaviour displayed by the survivor. Adult survivors entering the household will usually be more able to control themselves than a child would, but may also exhibit some behaviours that children may find difficult to understand or may even find frightening.

Wherever possible, try to explain to existing children as much of what is going on as possible. There is no need to go into the details of any abuse or be too specific. A simple statement such as explaining that the new arrival has been hurt by someone, and is not very well sometimes as a result of this, is often sufficient and is usually understandable by even quite young children. If nothing at all is said, children may imagine all sorts of things and sometimes may even end up feeling in some way responsible for what is going on in the house.

Children are young, not stupid, and will notice behaviour that is not normal to them. Things such as a survivor being very afraid, having flashbacks and mood swings, dissociation and any of the other things that survivors sometimes experience in different ways, may be noticed and commented on by children. Although children will not have the knowledge or experience to know or understand what any of these things are, they will certainly know that something strange is going on. It is usually better to make the children aware to some degree and acknowledge what they are noticing rather than ignoring it or trying to hide it from them. Flashbacks, for example can be explained by letting the child know that sometimes people who have been hurt remember being hurt and get frightened. Simple explanations usually work best.

It can be a good idea to also let a child know what they can do to help. Children cannot be expected to be quiet all the time but often the noises that children make while playing can be distressing for a survivor particularly squealing and screaming. Sometimes it is appropriate to ask a child to play a bit more quietly as the survivor is feeling ill. Children can be very keen to help if they know what will help and a small thing like encouraging a quiet game for a small time can help the child to feel included in helping out. At the same time, even although there are things that are distressing for the survivor, they have to learn to cope with normal life. Avoiding normal situations all the time will not help them in the long-term.

A great deal of time needs to be devoted to the care of survivors, particularly when they first escape from the abuse. This can easily lead to the children taking a back seat if a carer is not careful, especially as it is all too easy to get caught up in the crisis that the survivor is experiencing. Although it is difficult, carers have to try to divide their time and attention as equally as possible. Sometimes they will have to just leave the survivor suffering in order to see to the children. Survivors can be told quite clearly and will accept that others need attention too and even though you are leaving them alone for a while, you will be back and you do care about them.

Another thing that can help is getting in some outside help. Friends can help if they are inclined to by providing simple things such as respite care, going shopping and being there to listen when the carer needs to sound off. Help can also be sought from voluntary and statutory organisations in the shape of a befriender for the survivor, a counsellor, a social worker or a community psychiatric nurse. Although there is not a great deal of support or help available, there is some and it is worth the search if you eventually find help.

⇨ **In time survivors need their independence**. They need to be encouraged to trust other people, make new friends and begin to develop their own ways of coping and living in this world. Self-sufficiency and independence should be the main aim even though at first a survivor of any age may be very dependent on the people around them. Such dependence is normal. Survivors of ritual abuse have seldom been able to depend on anyone before and need to be able to do so at first without feeling that they are useless or a burden. Once they begin to feel more secure, they will no longer wish to be dependent on anyone.

People often feel as though they want to wrap the survivor up in cotton wool and protect them from the big bad world but while, at first, for a short time, this may help the survivor feel safe, it is not beneficial for them in the longer term. Survivors are strong and capable people who have been hurt and who can recover and move on. It is too late to protect them from all the evils of the world as they have already experienced these for themselves. What they need most when they get out of abuse is to become as independent as they possibly can and learn how to live their own lives. They should never have to do this alone.

Supporters of ritual abuse survivors need to learn when it is time to let go of any control they have and allow the survivor to spread their wings. Though this will be a scary time for all concerned, as there may be fears that the survivor is not strong enough or may return to the abuse, the survivor has a right to gain independence. It is not very different from watching your children grow up and beginning to venture out into the world. Supporters and carers can still be there for the survivor, but they must remember whose life it is.

Sometimes there is a need to gently push survivors to begin to explore the world. Some may become so immersed in the safety of their new home that they are not keen to face the world. This does not lead to independence and gentle encouragement to go out, make friends and generally begin to develop their personal skills can help. The trick is to take it slowly and gently but keep a hold of the fact that people have a right to as much independence as they can manage. You may not always be there for them even if you want to be. It is not beneficial for either the survivor or the supporter to be the only person that a survivor can trust. The more people involved in support and the greater the pool of people that the survivor can call upon in an emergency allows for greater independance.

**DUNDEE YOUNG WOMEN'S CENTRE**

# Chapter 16
# Safety First

Chapter 16
**Safety First**

**The first consideration when dealing with any type of abuse always ought to be safety.** Abuse necessarily involves abusers and these people are more than capable of doing violence to others and of placing people in danger. Obviously the safety of the survivor will be an important consideration for anyone encountering abuse, particularly on-going abuse. Other considerations may be; are there any children who might be in danger? With ritual abuse it is fairly certain that there will always be children who are at risk from the group. Whether or not you will ever be able to work out who these children actually are or do anything to help them is another issue. The other safety matter that frequently arises in relation to ritual abuse, is the question surrounding the safety of workers, or people closely involved with the survivor.

All of these issues need to be considered when working with ritual abuse survivors (and, indeed, any other kind of survivor) and it is beneficial to consider these issues thoroughly before becoming too involved with the survivor. In some cases you will already be involved before realising that the person is a survivor. Even if this is the case, it does not hurt to think things through and talk to someone about the issue of safety. The worst thing you could possibly do to a survivor is to make promises you cannot keep further down the line because of what the survivor starts to tell you.

I would emphasise that, in my experience, survivors themselves do not usually present any higher risk to a worker or anyone else's personal safety than anyone else in society, but thinking things through properly in advance can help the survivor more in the longer term. Addressing issues of safety in a frank and open manner usually achieves clarity.

Sometimes after building a relationship of trust with a survivor, they begin to be able to say more about the abuse. At that point, occasionally people get very freaked out by the things they start to hear and it is common for workers and others who have not thought things through at the start to begin to feel unsafe. Sometimes the feeling of not being safe comes from the fear that the survivor is feeling and on occasions it comes from hearing, sometimes for the first time, about the terrible things that the abusers are capable of doing to other people.

Sometimes too, the abusers find out that a survivor is talking and try to get to the survivors to silence them again. It has been known for survivors who have finally begun to talk after years of silence to be attacked by the abusers. At the same time it has been known for abusers to attempt to frighten off any supporters of the survivor in order to isolate them from help.

## Safety of Survivors ➢

Survivors, even after they escape from the group, rarely ever feel safe from the abusers. In reality, their fears are well justified, as the abusers will go to great lengths to make sure that survivors cannot tell and that if they do they will be completely disbelieved and discredited. Given that the abusers' greatest asset is the fact that few people believe that ritual abuse even happens, there is a good chance that any survivor trying to tell will not be believed anyway. These abusers, like men who commit acts of domestic violence, are often credible, likeable and ordinary people who would never be seen publicly to behave abusively towards other people. Everything they do is hidden from public view. This means that despite the very understandable fears of survivors, abusers are very unlikely to publicly harm a survivor. Such an act would simply make the invisible visible.

That is not to say that survivors who have managed to get out of the situation are then safe. It simply means that the abusers tend to use subtle tactics to maintain the silence and get the survivors back into the group. Such is the fear and conditioning of many survivors, that often they return when told. They may be too afraid to resist the command or totally conditioned to return to the group when ordered, particularly at set times. Once back, the abusers can reinforce the fear and conditioning. Due to the high degree of secrecy associated with ritual abuse, the safest survivor is the rare one who succeeds in telling about the group and the abuse officially and publicly. Though they may not be believed in what they are saying, if anything actually happens to them, the finger of suspicion will possibly be pointed in the right direction. Abusive groups will not usually risk exposure and tend to leave the more public survivors alone.

Many survivors talk about how they have been found again by their abusers even after many changes of identity and address. The same thing happens frequently with domestic abuse. Survivors who have been tracked down by the abusers are often frightened or coerced into going back. Although changing their name and address can help in the short term as it provides a bit breathing space, survivors find it difficult to disappear completely and need to be able to find other strategies to prevent the abusers from finding them and getting to them.

Survivors can do quite a lot to protect themselves by making sure that supportive people know where they should be and the time they should be there. They can, for example, arrange to have regular checking in times with other people, even by phone. They can write down incriminating information and lodge it with a friend or lawyer. The main trick is to make themselves accounted for by others. They should instruct people they know in how they should react in the event they do not check in as arranged. A call to the local police would get the best and quickest result. In this way, if the abusers do find a way to get to the survivor, the abusers are less likely to be able to make them disappear. In reality, many groups will just focus on tactics of fear and intimidation to keep control of the survivor, but anything at all that makes a survivor feel safer is worthy of a try.

Children who have somehow managed to get out of the group will feel very unsafe for a very long time. With good safe adults in their lives to protect them though, they are unlikely to be at risk from anyone in the group. They may receive letters, presents or cards from time to time, which appear on the surface to be very innocent. If, however, the child on receiving anything from anyone in their past, shows extremes of fear or reacts strangely to these items, there is probably a hidden message in it. The best way of dealing with this is to learn what to let them have and what to keep from them. Obviously, anything coming from any source that has upset them in the past ought to be kept from them. In time, as they grow stronger, they may be able to tell safe adults about the true meaning behind presents, cards or messages they are sent.

Some young people and adults who have escaped go back to their group when instructed as they have been told that someone will suffer if they do not return. Sometimes, survivors will reveal that the abusers have control of a child of theirs and threats are made against this child if they do not return. It is extremely hard for the survivor to realise that they have no power at all in this situation and if there is a child, the abusers can and will do what they want regardless of whether the survivor returns.

Even if there is no child but the survivor has been told there is, and has some reason to believe it might be possible, the survivor returns to the group believing they are saving the child from harm. In truth, the safest thing the survivor can do is sit it out and not go back. If there were a child believed to be at risk, the best people to deal with this would be the police. Having said that, in these circumstances, not one survivor, in my experience, would ever consider going forward to the police.

Survivors, especially those few who do go to the police, have to be very guarded about what they say. All survivors of this abuse will have been involved in committing a crime at some point in their lives, or will believe that they have. Survivors who escaped while very young, are exempt from prosecution if they disclose about the abuses that they were involved in, happened to them and that they were a witness to. However, anyone over the age of criminal responsibility, could face prosecution. Despite the fact that many survivors were still children at the time, or were forced to do things they didn't want to do, or had no understanding of what they were doing, any attempt to tell the whole truth to the police could lead to them facing prosecution.

There would be no understanding of the complexity of the survivors' position in the group or even that sometimes, faced with terrible, no win situations, the survivor may be forced to do things they do not want to. For example, the survivor may feel they have to hurt a child to try and save the child from greater hurt from the group, or to save other children by hurting just one. Survivors are faced regularly with issues such as these. In the end, few can consistently keep on refusing to do as they are told particularly, when the children themselves begin to blame him or her for the increased pain that they are suffering. The survivor quickly learns that, if they hurt one child they will save all the children from a great deal of suffering. Most survivors will have been faced with this type of situation since they were very young.

To stay safe, the survivor cannot always tell their full story to anyone, as many agencies would have to deal with the fact that this person before them has 'technically' abused a child. Even many rape crisis centres, which give good confidentiality for women can struggle with this as they work with people who are survivors, not abusers. While I do not consider the survivor in this situation to be an abuser, many who do not fully understand how the group dynamics of abuse work might see a person in that light. This would not be helped by the fact that most survivors in this situation feel very guilty and blame themselves for such abuses. This is of course exactly what the abusers intended. Survivors in this situation have absolutely no choice. They are merely the weapons used by the abusers.

## Safety of Workers and other Adults ➢

Workers and adults dealing with any type of abuse have to consider their own personal safety. They have to do this, not just in the sense of physical safety but also in terms of their emotional safety. This is because abusers sometimes are so desperate to stop the survivor from getting support and maintaining the silence that they will try to frighten off those who would be willing to help. Having said that, some abusers will usually try exceedingly hard to pretend to the outside world that they are good upstanding people and will, therefore, do nothing openly to jeopardise this view. Workers and supportive adults are perfectly safe from these types of people.

Some abusers however, will go to great lengths to get the survivor back and frighten off the supporter. In cases such as this, workers and supportive people have to be very careful. Some abusers do not like the fact that their 'victim' is being taken away from them and can respond with threats, violence and abuse against the person or persons helping the survivors. Often the form this takes is a low level harassment with threatening and abusive phone calls, being followed and harassed, or verbal abuse. Though none of these are directly an attack, they can be very frightening for the worker and supporters. All such threats and actions from an abuser should still be taken seriously. Workers need to make sure that they are well supported at work and able to let other workers and managers know that this sort of thing is happening. Other supporters too, need to let the people around them know that this is happening. Calling the police and making a complaint really ought to be the first thing that anyone does in this type of situation.

Occasionally, but more rarely, abusers do go further if they can and may try to actually assault a worker. Sometimes this takes the form of such actions as attempting to run the car off the road or interfering with car brakes or steering. This is of course potentially dangerous. Though abusers have been known very rarely to physically attack supporters, seldom has this happened in a public way. It is quite easy to become paranoid when working with a survivor especially if low-level harassment begins.

## Workers and supporters can stay safe by taking some basic personal safety steps such as:

- ▸▸ Making sure that friends and colleagues know their movements and checking in with them at pre-arranged times.

- ▸▸ Reporting any threats, abusive behaviour or harassment to the police immediately.

- ▸▸ Reporting any attacks on self or property to the police immediately.

- ▸▸ Telling friends and colleagues of any suspicions of danger, no matter how vague the suspicion seems.

- ▸▸ Telling the police and colleagues who you believe to be behind any risk to personal safety.

- ▸▸ Staying as public as possible.

Agencies, particularly those which provide home visits, ought to have a workers safety policy in place, which is adhered to at all times. Training ought to be provided for all workers regarding personal safety and this should be updated regularly. In addition to this, there ought to be adequate support and supervision in place for all workers who are working with survivors.

In order for workers to continue to adequately support survivors of ritual abuse, they need to learn to take care of themselves emotionally. The stories that are told by survivors can be difficult to hear and workers often need support and someone to offload to, in order to continue to cope with the things that they are hearing.

## Personal and Professional Credibility ➤

When anyone of any age begins to disclose that they have been ritually abused, the vast majority of people initially respond with disbelief and horror. Sometimes, particularly with a child disclosing abuse to an adult, the adult immediately contacts the police. Most people usually have an expectation that the police will simply sort everything out, investigate the matter and go off and arrest all of the abusers. On other occasions, social services are contacted and again most people have an expectation that it will all be sorted out. Unfortunately allegations of ritual abuse are not that easy to deal with or sort out.

For a start, no one quite believes that this type of abuse goes on in the first place, especially in his or her own area. On top of that, if the survivor tells the finer detail of what occurred during the abuse, a lot of what they have to tell sounds unbelievable. This is especially true of children. With children, the first thought that most people have is that they must be fantasising and making up stories. The way that children tell can add to the sense of disbelief. A child might say something along the lines of 'a big monster hurt me' and this sounds incredible. Though the child might give detail about what the 'monster' did, they often do not have the language or understanding to describe what really happened. Older children might be able to tell that the 'monster' was really a man wearing a costume and mask and thus shed some light on the matter. However, it is rare to find, in the first instance, people who will be able to give credence to the child's story. Though it might become apparent that the child has been abused, the child's story of what happened is just too far fetched.

With adults, the first thought that most people have is that the person telling the story has serious mental health problems. Given that many survivors do have mental health problems due to the severity of their abuse some, may regard what they are trying to tell as part of their medical condition. Unfortunately, the post traumatic stress experienced by many survivors can also mean that they suffer from hallucinations, delusions, paranoia and extreme anxiety attacks. While this certainly does not mean that what they are telling is not true, many people will judge the survivor to be a less than credible witness. It is much easier for people hearing about ritual abuse to believe in children's fantasy and mental health problems being the cause of 'a story' rather than believe that such things as ritual abuse actually do happen.

The next big problem is the one of evidence. Given that very few survivors are ever able to talk at the time of the abuse and often many years have gone past since it all happened, evidence of the crime is difficult to find. While hard and irrefutable evidence is certainly needed for conviction of any criminals, most victims of crimes do not have to prove irrefutably that the crime happened to them in the first place, before it is investigated thoroughly. Burglaries, muggings and thefts are all readily accepted and the survivors of these crimes are dealt with, with sympathy and compassion. These days most professionals even take domestic abuse and rape complaints seriously with sometimes the only evidence available at first being the distress and fear of the survivor. These complaints, without further evidence, may not get to the court, but at least the survivor is treated in a manner consistent with being believed and they are encouraged to make statements to the police.

Survivors of ritual abuse are quite simply not believed when they try to talk. Immediately on saying the 'unbelievable', many professionals are fairly quickly asking them to prove it to them and doubting what is being said. It has to be said that not all professionals behave like this, but certainly the vast majority do. Though this is from the perspective of the survivor totally unacceptable and very off-putting, it is, at the same time perfectly understandable.

# Where Angels Fear

Imagine the situation of a police officer that succeeds in moving past their own initial disbelief and listens to survivors, takes seriously all that the survivor is saying to them and promises to investigate the crime. This officer will then have to face colleagues and superiors who still do not believe that ritual abuse happens and will ridicule the officer for believing the unbelievable. The police officer would need to take a lot of time both in talking to the survivor and beginning the search for the elusive evidence for crimes that the police do not believe possible. The chances of the officer being allowed to continue for long on such a perceived wild goose chase are slim.

In addition to this, the police officer, along with anyone else who believes what the survivor is saying will lose credibility. The assumption will be that at best they are gullible and at worst completely crazy for believing the unbelievable. The chances of promotion tend to go right out the window for any officer who believes such abuse happens. Then, if the press gets hold of as much as a whisper that ritual abuse is being investigated, everything gets blown out of all proportion and the police force in the area are thoroughly discredited and castigated. The press rarely stick to the real facts and tend to dramatise and ridicule all accounts of ritual abuse.

Many professionals, brave or stupid enough to try and make a public stand on the issue of ritual abuse, have lost their credibility and some have even lost their jobs. Social services and voluntary organisations have had their fingers burned so badly on a number of cases they tried to investigate in Britain, that few would now openly admit to believing such abuse possible, let alone want to investigate it. In reality, it is usually committing professional suicide to enter the realms of ritual abuse without hard evidence at hand. Yet, no one can ever get hard evidence unless they first look into the matter.

Interestingly, despite the huge and sustained backlash of the press, the tide is beginning to turn with more and more ordinary people beginning to wonder about ritual abuse. It is more likely now that ordinary people, on hearing about ritual abuse, will respond by thinking that there is something in it. Whether this is to do with a belief that there is no smoke without fire, or whether more people have become accustomed to reading about child sexual abuse and domestic abuse in the press and are therefore more likely to believe that abusers might go further, I do not know. It is still a case though that most professionals are very reluctant to take it on.

By far the best way to get police and social services on board with survivors of ritual abuse is to get the survivor to steer clear of talking about the ritualistic parts of the abuse at first. If survivors need to approach these agencies, talking in the first instance about physical and sexual violence will at least get the survivor a hearing. Once there is more of a relationship, the survivor can go on and talk about the rest and stands more chance of being believed. Many survivors do this anyway as they know that it is unlikely they will be believed about some aspects of their abuse.

Agencies and workers are not to blame for finding ritual abuse stories difficult to believe. This attitude merely reflects the culture of disbelief and denial that is prevalent in this country. It also reflects the lessons learned through seeing colleagues and other agencies getting their fingers burned through listening to and believing survivors. Cases involving ritual abuse often become so high profile that they are swiftly taken up by the media who inevitably ridicule and sensationalise every aspect of the case. The main message that the press puts out time and time again is that ritual abuse does not happen and professionals are gullible and involved in the witch hunting of poor innocents. The result of this is that in any case involving ritual abuse, for it to succeed in getting to court, this aspect of the abuse has to be played down and the case be taken forward as 'straight forward' abuse. Juries tend to reflect the view of society and would have the same problem as everyone else in believing the unbelievable.

Somewhere along the line, people need to start wondering why it is that survivors, despite the disbelief of the world, still continue to maintain the truth of what they are saying? They achieve nothing at all from this except disbelief, denial and being labelled as crazy. People also need to start questioning why it is that the media, particularly the popular press, are so eager to discount all possibility of ritual abuse and deny its existence while increasingly promoting pornography in their publications? Perhaps the other unpopular question that needs to be asked is why, in investigations of ritual abuse, statutory workers dealing with the investigation are frequently unsupported, silenced and whenever things get difficult, i.e. the press gets hold of it, they lose all credibility and even their jobs?

Some workers from a variety of agencies, end up being treated by society in the same way as the ritual abuse survivors and become the 'survivors of daring to believe that ritual abuse may happen'. You do not have to look far in this country to find the workers from agencies who have been the scapegoats and have become the casualties of the ritual abuse backlash. Such is the determination of some people to deny any possibility of ritual abuse and stop any investigation into it at every opportunity, that anyone daring to side with survivors faces, at best, ridicule and loss of credibility. At worst, they are censored and sacked. Why, if ritual abuse does not happen and does not exist, are some people so fiercely hostile in their opposition? Why put so much energy into a fight against something that is not there?

Chapter 17
# After-word

Chapter 17
**After-word**

**I wrote this book over a two-week period and am told that it just stops dead. It does, because I ran out of spare time and just stopped writing it**. I was going to put in a survivors perspective at the end as I did in my previous book, but on looking back through the contents of the book, decided that the perspective of survivors infiltrates the whole book. Throughout, I have attempted to ensure that survivors are central to the subject. At the same time, I have been constantly guided by survivors and have passed by survivors, every word written for their comments and approval.

Once again I would like to reiterate that no survivor's confidentiality has been broken and any experiences provided in this book are provided with the full consent and knowledge of the individuals concerned. If any of the details or events printed in this book are in any way similar to another person's experience, this is pure coincidence. Honestly, I do not read minds!

Rather than a foreword, an after-word seems more appropriate for this book. It is always difficult to know or anticipate what other people want and need to know about any given subject. It is also impossible to know what prior knowledge people have and this can vary so widely depending on experience. Having written this book and then passed a draft to several people for comments, it has become clear that much more needs to be said on the subject of ritual abuse than I have said here or in my previous book. For some, this book will not be in-depth enough and for others, there will be too much assumed.

Throughout the book it has been difficult to find the right words to describe some events and I have deliberately chosen to be vague about some of the details (events and implements) so as to try and protect any survivors who might read this book. Survivors know their own details already and other people will just have to try to use their imagination or even ask me directly if they want to know any more.

I was asked to tone the book down a bit and have done so in order to reduce the chances of a lawsuit. I was also asked to make the book more credible by leaving some things out of it. The first I did by removing some of the details that would identify some of the abusers. Their time will come! The second I did not do. Survivors have the right to be heard no matter how incredible their experiences may sound to others and maybe people need to find a way of just getting their heads round it.

If there is anything readers would like to have explained further or would like more information about, feel free to contact me through the Young Women's Centre. I will not share with anyone any details about any survivors or their personal experience, but I am happy to share any knowledge or experience that I have on the subject of ritual abuse. Though I know a little, I am no expert and certainly do not know everything. Survivors are the experts on their own experiences. I will share what I can though.

Before you contact me to ask for explanations, try reading my first book 'Who Dares Wins' as the answers might well be in there. Otherwise, there are many other books available on the subject, which may enlighten you.

Feel free to send me feedback or comments on any of my books. Though I cannot promise to write back to everyone (a stamped addressed envelope will help), if enough people want to know more about a particular subject, I could always write about it and explain a bit more in book three. I have always wanted to write a trilogy!

# Where Angels Fear

This book has been written to try and help survivors of ritual abuse by enlightening people about the subject and suggesting ways of helping survivors. I hope that there is nothing contained in this book that will upset any survivors but I would write nothing at all if I avoided all possible triggers. Even writing about the subject will be upsetting for some. If any survivors who on reading this book, find anything upsetting, I apologise wholeheartedly for this. It is not the survivors I want to upset, rather I would prefer to upset those people who choose to abuse power in this manner.

Some survivors may find some of the things I have spoken about upsetting as they have been conditioned not to talk about or reveal these things to anyone. Hopefully, survivors, through knowing that others have broken the silence, talked to me and allowed and encouraged me to write, and still survived, will gain strength from this book. The other hope I have, is that the abusers will realise that their secrets are not as safe as they thought they were. Survivors can, and do, eventually grow strong and tell. In time, more and more people will listen.

*This book is hereby dedicated to the colour* **GREY!**

# Other Titles by
# Vip Publications

| Subject | Title | Price | | Postage |
|---------|-------|-------|---|---------|
| **Abuse Prevention** | **Teen Vip Training Pack:** | £55.00 | plus | £5.00 p&p |
| | **Jenny's Story** | £6.50 | plus | £0.50 p&p |
| | **Wee Vip Pack:** Game, Story, Video. | £95.00 | plus | £5.00 p&p |
| | **Jonny Cool:** Storybook | £10.00 | plus | £1.50 p&p |
| | **Jonny Cool:** Workbook | £5.00 | plus | £1.50 p&p |
| | **Jonny Cool:** Workbook & Storybook | £15.00 | plus | £5.00 p&p |
| **Games** | **Truth! Dare! Scare!:** Safety Game | £55.00 | plus | £5.00 p&p |
| **Poetry Books** | **Hear We are again** | £3.50 | plus | £0.50 p&p |
| | **Listen! Hear!** | £3.50 | plus | £0.50 p&p |
| | **Hear! We are!** | £3.50 | plus | £0.50 p&p |
| | **Hear! Us!** | £3.50 | plus | £0.50 p&p |
| **StoryTime Series** | 1,2 or 3 | £5.00 ea. | plus | £1.50 p&p |
| **Music** | **After the Storm** CD | £10.00 | plus | £5.00 p&p |
| | **After the Storm** T-shirt | £6.50 | plus | £1.50 p&p |
| **Information** | **Postcards** (8) | £3.50 | plus | £0.50 p&p |
| | **Information Booklets** | Free | plus | £0.50 p&p |
| **Books** | **Who Dares Wins!** Ritual Abuse book | £15.00 | plus | £5.00 p&p |
| | **BeAware:** Supporting Young Surivors of Abuse book | £15.00 | plus | £5.00 p&p |
| | **Where Angels Fear** Ritual Abuse book | £15.00 | plus | £5.00 p&p |

**All these publications are available from:**

Young Women's Centre,
1 Victoria Road, Dundee, DD1 1EL
Telephone: 01382 206 222

Please make cheques payable to "Dundee Young Women's Centre (Trading) Ltd"
Please enclose remittance to the value of the cover price plus the cost shown for postage
and packing. Applicable only in the UK. Overseas prices on application. Prices are subject
to change without notice.